With All Our Prayers

Walking with God
through the Christian Year

John B. Rogers Jr.

WILLIAM B. EERDMANS PUBLISHING COMPANY
GRAND RAPIDS, MICHIGAN / CAMBRIDGE, U.K.

Published 2015 by
Wm. B. Eerdmans Publishing Co.
2140 Oak Industrial Drive N.E., Grand Rapids, Michigan 49505 /
P.O. Box 163, Cambridge CB3 9PU U.K.

Printed in the United States of America

20 19 18 17 16 15   7 6 5 4 3 2 1

Library of Congress Cataloging-in-Publication Data

Rogers, John B., 1941-
With all our prayers: walking with God through the Christian year /
John B. Rogers, Jr.
pages   cm
ISBN 978-0-8028-7191-6 (pbk.: alk. paper)
1. Pastoral prayers. 2. Prayers. 3. Church year — Prayers and devotions.
4. Public worship.   I. Title.

BV250.R65   2015
264'.13 — dc23

2014040381

www.eerdmans.com

With All Our Prayers

For Addison Lane
with much affection
From Rebeca and Dean Thompson
October 2017
We believe in you!

Contents

Preface

The traditional biblical teaching that human beings are created "in the image of God" is rooted in, and is witness to, the unique relationship God has established with humanity. Theologians and others have long sought to identify some particular attribute or quality humans possess as that which constitutes God's image in us; for example: reason, imagination, the capacity for self-transcendence whereby we are able to regard ourselves as objects, to observe and to judge ourselves.

The book of Genesis, however, seems to say that the "image of God" is not anything human beings possess. Rather, it rests solely upon what God decides about us, and what God does with and for us. In these profound stories of human origin and purpose, God speaks personally to the human creatures, establishing with them a relationship unlike any other. Addressed by God's word of creation and command, we are called to respond, to answer. Human beings are "the praying animals" (Robert Jenson). Made "in the image of God," we are creatures who pray.

Most of the prayers in this collection were offered during worship at Covenant Presbyterian Church in Charlotte, North Carolina. As "Prayers of the People," or pastoral prayers, they contain the traditional elements of adoration, confession, thanksgiving, intercession (prayers for others and for the world), and petition (prayers for ourselves). Additionally, these prayers focus somewhat more intentionally on issues of faith, and on pastoral situations in a congregation, in a community, and in the lives of individuals and families. They are intended to invite all readers — whether pastors, churches, small groups, or individuals — to take an intentional journey with God through the Christian year.

I am deeply grateful for the faith of the women and men, the youth and children in four congregations whom it has been my privilege to serve as pastor. They have prayed for me, and have helped me to pray with and for them.

Three treasured friends are due special thanks: Dean K. Thompson, fellow laborer in the vineyard of parish ministry and former president of Louisville Presbyterian Theological Seminary, whose initiative and encouragement led to the publication of this volume; Sally Graves, for her careful preparation of this manuscript, her helpful suggestions along the way, and her competence, creativity, good cheer, and patience throughout the process; and Martha Isaacs, for her thoughtful reading of these prayers with a worshiper's eye and ear.

JOHN B. ROGERS JR.

Introduction: With All Our Prayers

In the name of the Father, and of the Son, and of the Holy Spirit, let us pray: We come to you in prayer, Eternal God, able to do so because you have first come to us, and daring to do so because, having created us for yourself, claimed us for your own possession, and called us to be your covenant people, you have made the gift of prayer a defining mark of our life with you. You have revealed to us your name so that we know to whom we pray. You have called us by name so that we may pray with confidence that we are known of you and that we matter to you both presently and ultimately. Just so do our prayers express our faith born of your faithfulness. Just so are they our trusting words in answer to your sovereign Word uttered from the foundation of the world, living and active to accomplish your promised salvation and to bear your righteous command, and incarnate in Jesus Christ our Lord. By his grace, and in the fellowship of the Holy Spirit, our lives are anchored in your love and hidden securely in your own triune life. Wherefore we come to you with all our prayers.

Amen.

I Am

(The prayer begins with a period of silence.)

Let us pray: Eternal God, before we speak, even in prayer, we must listen. We must listen for you to break the silence of eternity, for you to speak from beyond us a word of your presence with us and of our nearness to you. We remember that the universe exists because you spoke it into being, saying, "Let there be light, order, heavens and earth" . . . and it was so. We remember that we are because you created us male and female in your image. We remember that from of old you told us your name: "I Am . . . I Am Who I Will Be . . . I Am The One Who Will Be Present With You, For You, Among You As God." Your name is your promise — your Word that makes room in your life for us. And now, on the threshold of Advent, we would prepare our hearts and our homes for the coming of him who bears your name, who is your promise in person, your Word made flesh — even Jesus Christ our Lord.

We are grateful, O God, for all that Christ's coming reveals to us about you, about this world, about ourselves. We give thanks that to know Jesus Christ, dwelling among us full of grace and truth, is to know you, your mind toward us, your love of us, your will for us.

As we enter upon this Advent season, help us to welcome and not resist Christ's coming, to prepare and not to impede his way toward and among us. Let it not be:

that we know the burden of our sin, but do not greet our Savior;
that we nurture our resentments and enmities, but fail to
welcome the Prince of Peace who gives us the ministry of
reconciliation;
that we remain prisoners of loneliness while he stands at the door
whose name is Emmanuel — God with us;
that we continue in discouragement and dark despair when the
light of the world has come that no darkness can withstand;
that we so quickly claim Christ to bless our small plans and priorities while we fail to discern in him your larger purpose for
the world;
that we pervert the Christmas message to a word of judgment
while we are deaf to the angels' song: good news of great joy
to all people.

How then do we make ready for Christ's coming, O God? We
could pray for our world, that suspicion, hatred, and violence might
be overcome by peace and good will; and we could pledge ourselves
to be instruments to that end. We could pray for our nation, that
those who govern and enact laws might have a heart for justice and
compassion and wise government that overrides personal ambition
and party interests; and we could become such citizens ourselves.
We could pray for our city, that people of faith and communities
of faith might, with gratitude and humility, follow the best light of
their religious traditions in the treatment of those who are different, and in the building up of the common life; and we could do
that ourselves in the very name of Jesus Christ. We could pray for
ourselves, our own families, and friends that the spirit of Christ
might so adorn our witness that others, whatever their faith, will be
glad for the birth of him whose name we bear, and in whose name
we worship and pray and serve. O God, none of this will cause or
prevent Christ's coming — we know that. But it might make us
more faithful and effective as those to whom you have given the

responsibility to prepare his way, to announce his advent, and to feed his sheep. Even so, come Lord Jesus. And now, O God, hear us as we pray together the prayer Christ taught us . . .

Amen.

And His Name Shall Be Called Emmanuel, God with Us

Let us pray: Eternal God, Christmas approaches and we become more aware of your nearness to us, of your presence with us in the wondrous event of an infant's birth whose name, Emmanuel, God with us, echoes both the present certainty and the promised assurance of your own name: "I am the one who will be with you." We are struck by how the meaning of Christmas is contained in the name the child is given, and the ways he is addressed during his lifetime:

"Jesus" — God is our salvation — that supreme good news set before us in his person;

"Christ" — the anointed one who ushers in the kingdom of God, your own rule of grace in and over all of life;

"Rabbi" — who as our teacher opens to us your Word that reads and interprets us, commands and directs us;

"Good Shepherd" — who knows his sheep by name, even those who are not of our fold;

"The True Vine" — into whom we are grafted as branches, and in whose life and strength we are able to bear the fruit of obedience and service, justice and righteousness, compassion and peace.

We are grateful for all that the "names" of Christmas convey to us of your love and grace, your purpose and power, your reassurance and redemption. The coming of Christmas rekindles in us the desire to experience your nearness so intensely that, with the psalmist, we may cry:

Thou dost beset me behind and before, and layest thy hand upon me. Such knowledge is too wonderful for me. . . . (Psalm 139:5-6, RSV)

In the midst of our Advent preparation this year, eternal God, in our hearts and in our homes and in this congregation, become real to us once again, we pray, and in the silence of our souls speak to us that we may open ourselves to your presence with us in Jesus Christ our Lord.

As we bring to you our petitions and intercessions, gracious God, let us be honest with you and say to you what is on our hearts. Some of us are here in what can only be called a rebellious spirit and with grievances that make us ill at ease in our prayer: help us to be forthright in bringing our complaints and resentments before you and to speak frankly to you about them. If we have been ill-treated or have been done some injustice, help us to express our feelings to you and not just keep things festering within. But neither let us dwell upon our complaints that they be all we express. Rather, let us remain long enough in prayer for your healing hand to be laid upon us and your wisdom to bring to us perspective and understanding so that, like a storm-tossed sea when the wind dies down, our anxious and turbulent spirits may grow quiet in the security of your peace.

Some of us come before you, O God, with sin in our lives for which we are not remorseful, but with which, instead, we have grown comfortable. Here too we must be honest with you: about commandments ignored, trusts betrayed, relationships violated, truths compromised. Even so, help us to remain long enough in your presence for you to shine the light of your grace upon us in the face of Christ whose advent we await, that his way of life might draw us back from the foolish and self-defeating ways we have chosen into the way that leads to life.

Some of us come before you in need of courage. Many of us who are outwardly placid and comfortable are inwardly discouraged and beaten and near the end of our rope. Life has come down hard upon some of us. Death has come roaring into our households and laid its chilling hand upon our hearts. There are friends who have disappointed us and loved ones who have hurt us, often without even knowing it. There have been disappointments at work and setbacks in those good causes to which we have given our energy. Many of us are anxious about our homes, our health, our children, our community. Let us remain long enough in prayer, O God, to hear you say to us: "Be not anxious. . . . Let not your hearts be troubled, neither let them be afraid."

Eternal God, you call us to and encourage us in lives not of ease, but of sufficiency. Send us forth from our worship and our prayers to be builders and servants of a better world. Our hearts are burdened in this place of beauty and of privilege by the poverty and pain that afflict so many. Your providence has been sufficient and more, and the world has brought forth abundantly so that all should be fed and housed, educated and valued. But something has gone wrong in our hearts and our relationships one with another such that some among us are hungry and homeless, ignorant and forgotten. Let us not be selfish in our privilege, O God. Challenge us to be both generous in giving of our resources and just in building a society that has an open heart and an open hand to those on whom life presses down the hardest. Make our own hearts sensitive and our consciences quick, lest our own ease dull our compassion for those who are your children every bit as much as we are, and for whom your heart breaks to see them suffer.

These and all our prayers we make in the name of him in whose birth are met the hopes and fears of all the years, even Jesus Christ our Lord, who taught us to pray . . .

Amen.

Good News of Great Joy ... to All People

The history of salvation begins with God's call and promise to Abraham: "I will bless you . . . and by you all the families of the earth shall bless themselves" (Gen. 12:2-3, RSV). Christmas declares that God's promise is fulfilled:

> The angel said to [the shepherds], "Be not afraid; for behold, I bring you good news of a great joy which will come to all the people; for to you is born this day in the city of David a Savior, who is Christ the Lord." (Luke 2:10-11, RSV)

Let us pray: Eternal God, whose promise to bless all the nations of the earth runs like a golden thread through your sovereign purpose, your mighty acts, and your hidden providence that marks the unfolding drama of the birth of Christ, we give thanks in this Advent season as we mark anew the fulfillment of that promise in the Holy Child of Bethlehem. We are grateful that Christmas begins in the pivotal event in history that is truly "good news of great joy . . . to all people." Thanks be to you, merciful God, that in Jesus Christ what is essential and definitive about the human family, and each member thereof, has been decided, declared, and disclosed. Thanks be to you that in this particular human life you have overcome all that separates human beings from you . . . our sinfulness from your holiness, our weak devotion from your steadfast love, our inveterate grasping from your invincible grace. Thanks be to you that you have claimed us as your own forever — a defining truth about us that we may deny, but that we can neither negate nor undo.

Give us ears to hear and hearts to understand Christmas as the astounding good news it is, O God . . . not as a deal we make or a bargain we control by our acceptance or rejection, but as the declaration of a love that will not let us go even when we struggle against it. And, O God, forbid that in our witness to others we make of this good news of Christmas a condition that must be satisfied, a threat to frighten, a weapon to coerce, a reason to condemn others. Let not those who have yet to hear of Christ miss the good news of great joy to all people because ours is a witness more of judgment than of grace, more of condemnation than of redemption, more of slim possibility held out than of accomplished joy to the world.

God of grace and truth, compassion and peace, righteousness and justice, for whom this world hungers and thirsts: let your Spirit rule among the nations in this season of good will, that mutual trust and open hearts may overcome suspicion, and that a desire to live and work together might overcome enmity and the violence it so often begets. Grant that the reconciliation you wrought in Jesus Christ may bind people with people, race with race, nation with nation, even creed with creed in a community of mutual care and understanding and concord.

Be with all who in this Christmas season will seek to bring happiness to others, and give to them joy and deep satisfaction in their tasks.

Let the light of the world that shines in the face of Christ fall on our several pathways that our homes may be radiant with love and loyalty and appreciation among husbands and wives and children, that our churches may increase their devotion, deepen their commitment, and strengthen their obedience to Christ and his kingdom by spending themselves in the service of those things that really matter, and not in such pursuits that trivialize the Gospel. And help us, in this church, we pray, to know the difference.

God of mercy, draw near to those in whose hearts there is little room for joy because sorrow has come so close to them and taken from them one beloved above all — a wife or husband, a son or daughter, a mother or father, a brother or sister, a friend or loved one. May the Christ who has heard their cries and been their help in need and their companion in joy now hold them close to himself to comfort and reassure. And in the knowledge of his love and care may they find peace that passes understanding. Indeed, may they find even joy that comes again to the world and all who dwell therein in the Holy Child of Bethlehem. So we believe, and so we pray:

O come, thou Dayspring, come and cheer our spirits
　　by thine advent here;
Disperse the gloomy clouds of night, and death's dark shadows
　　put to flight.
O come, Desire of nations, bind all peoples in one heart
　　and mind;
Bid envy, strife, and discord cease, fill the whole world
　　with heaven's peace.

("O Come, O Come, Emmanuel,"
Latin, c. 12th century; stanza 2:
trans. John Mason Neale, 1861; stanza 3: trans.
Henry Sloane Coffin, 1916)

These prayers we offer in the spirit of him whose name is called Emmanuel, God with us, and who taught us to pray . . .

Amen.

The Beyond in the Midst of Life

ADVENT

The letter to the Hebrews opens like a Gospel:

> Long ago God spoke to our ancestors in many and various ways by
> the prophets, but in these last days he has spoken to us by a Son.
> (Heb. 1:1-2a, NRSV)

Let us pray: Eternal God, as another Advent season comes to a
close and we draw near the manger, we are mindful that it is because
you came to us in Jesus Christ that we can come to you in his name
with all our prayers . . . that in Christ you have taken our humanity
upon yourself in order to make a place for us within your own life
and heart. All this is of your free and sovereign grace set visibly
before us in a tiny infant born of Mary.

We are grateful for those times of blessing when, in a quiet moment alone, or at worship — in the beauty of an anthem, in the
poetry of a familiar carol, in the silence of the Sacrament, in a sud-
den insight that seizes our minds — the sheer, shimmering wonder
of your birth among us breaks through the clamor of life and the
complacency of our hearts and wraps us in joy and gladness. O
God, help us to be open once again to such glimpses into the heart
of Christmas.

Hear now our intercessions, we pray, as we remember before you
all for whom we want to pray: bless and keep watch in our homes
and families that love, fidelity, and appreciation for one another

might strengthen the circle of family with lasting joy and well-being. Bless our friends, and those with whom we work. Grant to one and all the spirit of understanding and strength to do our duty gladly and well. Be near to those we think of who are sick, and to those we name in our hearts who are sad. Grant them comfort in their grief and a return to health and strength.

Bless this congregation of your people, O God, and all who lead and work and participate in its life, and all who sustain it by their presence and by their prayers, their gifts of talents and time and resources. Give to us in this church family that unity in Jesus Christ that makes us strong to witness to your love and goodness.

Bless the greater church, we pray: in our city, in our nation, the church universal, that in its message and mission it will offer words and work and witness that are clear and faithful and compelling.

Bless our nation, we pray: our president and all who are in positions of leadership who advise the president, and those who shape public opinion in our land, and the whole body of our people. Give us those qualities of mind and heart in our nation and in our city by which we will be strong to defend what is right, swift to protect the weak and the poor, eager to live at peace and with good will toward peoples of other nations.

Bless the community of nations in our world, O God, we pray. Look upon the turmoil and suspicion that are threatening the lives of so many in these days. Grant that nations of differing color and creed, language and politics may no longer be kept apart by prejudice and suspicion and hatred, but may together enjoy the riches of living together in good will, in mutual cooperation, and in a common desire for justice and peace.

Lord God, hear us now as we pray for those for whom we need to pray and must pray: those from whom we are estranged . . . those whom we have wronged . . . those against whom we bear some grudge . . . those about whom we are worried . . . those for whom we grieve . . . those for whom Christmas is hard — the poor who ache for what their children will not receive this year, the homeless who have no place to lay their head and call their own, those out of work who struggle just to make it through another day. We pray for those for whom this is likely their last Christmas. We pray for those who are so alone they believe they have no one to pray for them. Let our prayers express the desire of our hearts, that, through your grace and by our actions as your people, broken hearts may be mended with love, pain soothed by compassion, fear overcome with courage, and loneliness with companionship.

And now, O God, bring us along the final steps in our Advent journey until we stand beside the cradle of the Christ Child, and hear him say: "I am yours, and you are mine. . . . Let us put our lives together and be about the Father's business." So come to us once again, O God, and draw us anew into your life that with all our hearts we may know you, love you, and serve you through Jesus Christ our Lord, who taught us to pray . . .

Amen.

And the Word Became Flesh
and Dwelt among Us

Let us pray: Eternal God, the Apostle has declared:

For it is the God who said, "Let light shine out of darkness," who has shone in our hearts to give the light of the knowledge of the glory of God in the face of Jesus Christ. (2 Cor. 4:6, NRSV)

And so we come once more to peer into the manger and to behold the Child whose name is Emmanuel, God with us. The Gospel of Christ fills our grateful hearts: that you, O God, come to us as God in the person of Jesus Christ . . . that this event that happened centuries ago is not only the central event in history, but is the constitutive event of your own life . . . that you truly and definitively are who we know you to be in Christ, and not otherwise. So that now we must take seriously our own lives, and every life, as precious to you. And we must understand now that we are characters known, named, loved in a drama in which you yourself are with us, for us, and among us.

Help us, O God, on this Christmas Eve to be grasped in the depths of our hearts and at the top of our minds by the concreteness of the Gospel: that because you have joined your life to ours in Jesus Christ and gathered us into your life, nothing can separate us from your love or take us out of your hand . . . neither death nor life nor anything else in all creation. Help us to know this in a new and fresh way on this Christmas Eve, and, as we come to your table, help us to see and touch the One who meets us here full of grace, and who makes the Gospel true, even Jesus Christ our Lord.

Amen.

Mine Eyes Have Seen Thy Salvation

When Mary and Joseph presented the infant Jesus at the Temple, Luke tells us that old Simeon, a righteous and devout man, inspired by the Holy Spirit, took the child in his arms and sang:

> Lord, now lettest thou thy servant depart in peace, according to thy word; for mine eyes have seen thy salvation which thou hast prepared in the presence of all peoples, a light for revelation to the Gentiles, and for glory to thy people Israel. (Luke 2:29-31, RSV)

Simeon's song has since taken its place in the worship and hymnody of the church as the "Nunc Dimittis," and remains a treasured part of Christian liturgy. As we greet a new year with a mixture of eagerness and anxiety, hopes and fears about what the future may hold, this ancient canticle clarifies our vision and shines its light upon our praying.

Let us pray: Eternal God, as we mark the turning of a new year, we are grateful for Simeon's reminder that, in the One whose birth we celebrate in these days of Christmas, you have come in person to claim, as your own possession, our time and all time, our lives and all life.

Through Jesus Christ, deepen in us the realization that you are not an abstract, impersonal "something," but a particular Someone — God with us, God for us, God among us: Life to life, Spirit to spirit, Heart to heart. And in that knowledge inspire us to dedicate ourselves to the peace you would bring to the world's enmity; the reconciliation you would seek for our estrangements; the justice and righteousness you demand in our common life; the compassion and tenderness in which you hold and heal our brokenness; and the rule of grace and goodwill that is the kingdom of God. May this be our vocation and witness as your children and your church, O God, offered with open hearts and open arms in the name of Jesus Christ our Lord who, whatever the future holds, holds the future in the strong security of his steadfast love and invincible grace.

So we believe and so, as he taught us, we pray . . .

Amen.

The Light of the World

EPIPHANY

The prophet of the Exile spoke of the coming of the Light:

> Arise, shine; for your light has come, and the glory of the LORD has risen upon you. (Isa. 60:1, RSV)

The Fourth Gospel declares of Christ:

> The light shines in the darkness, and the darkness has not overcome it. (John 1:5, RSV)

Jesus said:

> I am the light of the world. Whoever follows me will never walk in darkness but will have the light of life. (John 8:12, NRSV)

Let us pray: Eternal God, everything speaks to us of light, of revelation, of truth made manifest, and understanding illumined. The music of the Christmas gospel still lingers in the air, announcing that the light that shines in the darkness has come to us and to all people. The season of Epiphany opens our minds to the significance of the Christ Child for the world. And so, in spite of the darkness around us and within us, we come with grateful hearts at the beginning of a new year to the table of Christ, here to take our spiritual bearings, to strengthen our faith, to orient our lives, to sustain our souls.

Where else could we begin, O God? We are grateful for glimpses of truth, for flashes of light, for pivotal events, for bits of wisdom that come to us from various disciplines, fields of study, life experiences, world religions, broadening relationships. All of these enrich us and help us to live life at a deeper level. But none of these is able, we confess, to withstand the darkness of life more than occasionally or in part. In none of these do you come to dwell in person among us.

Only in Jesus Christ do you meet us in the fullness of your life with us and for us. Only he is God incarnate — the light in which all lights are illumined. Only his life, death, and resurrection constitute the Event in light of which all other events are given meaning.

So as we hear the words of institution, and as we eat this bread and drink this cup, help us to become more aware of just what has happened to us and to this world in Jesus Christ. Help our minds and hearts to be seized anew by what you have declared, disclosed, demonstrated in Christ about your relationship to us and our belonging to you. And, O God, because we begin the year in communion with Christ, make us eager to live out of this good news; make us more willing for it to direct our treatment of others; make us more open and generous and gracious in our approach to the world. Make us more faithful in the things to which we are willing to commit ourselves: justice, compassion, graciousness, and good cheer. And make us more faithful as well in the things from which we are determined to withhold ourselves: self-righteousness, hard-heartedness, cruelty, and enmity. So feed us anew, O God, and fit us for your service in the new year, through Jesus Christ our Lord.

Amen.

Prayers from Deep Within

Psalm 130 begins with the words:

Out of the depths I cry to you, O LORD!

To his beloved Philippian congregation, soon to face the depths of Nero's persecution, Paul wrote:

> Have no anxiety about anything, but in everything by prayer and supplication with thanksgiving let your requests be made known to God. And the peace of God, which passes all understanding, will keep your hearts and your minds in Christ Jesus. (Phil. 4:6-7, RSV)

Let us pray: Once again, eternal God, we come in the order of worship to the Prayers of the People. The minister says, "Let us pray," and we bow our heads. We are grateful for the gift of prayer, but often we wonder: What should our prayers look like? For what should we pray? For whom should we pray? And how? We do not know! Deep inside ourselves, so often, we are a tangle of competing needs and desires, of hopes and fears such that we cannot sort them out into a coherent prayer. Can we just lay ourselves open to you in all our confusion and in the emotional and spiritual complexity that besets us, and trust that you can sort it out and help us deal with it? You know us, O God: to you all hearts are open, all desires known, and from you no secrets are hid. Where we are tense with anxiety, help us to relax in the assurance of your presence and your eagerness to help us. Where we are trying to solve a problem, give us wisdom and perspective and understanding. Where resentment has taken hold of us, deliver us from self-pity and from the acid of bitterness that eats away at the soul and makes us sour and surly. Where guilt and shame weigh on us, help us to ask for forgiveness and to experience the lifting of the burden and the joy of reconciliation. Where life is putting us to the test, where responsibilities press upon us, where decisions have to be made, help us to apply our clearest thinking, our best abilities, our best efforts in the stewardship entrusted to us, through Jesus Christ our Lord.

For all that we do not know about how to pray, O God, we do know that we ourselves cannot be the center of all our prayers . . . that we should, that we must pray for others. Even here we usually start close to ourselves and pray for those we love and those we know and like: faces come easily to mind and names fall easily from our tongues as we pray for fathers and mothers, husbands and wives, sons and daughters, brothers and sisters, those in the circles of family and faith and friendship. We think of those who are ill and those who are anxious for them: keep them close to your heart in their pain and fear, and work in them your healing power. We remember those whose pain is more than physical, and deeper, and more persistent and unremitting. Meet them, O God, and stand with them and hold them in those deep places of pain and grief. And help us to sustain them where appropriate with our kind and thoughtful words, but also with our loving presence, our understanding silences. Help us to be more sensitive than we usually are to the needs of others, that by our willingness to be with them, to bear with them in their suffering, and to let them grieve while we stand back and stand by and wait, we may give comfort to broken hearts and lift broken spirits.

There are prayers for others that do not come quite so easily to speech, O God: prayers for people we do not love or like or know; strangers, people of a different race, a different faith, a different culture, different opinions and commitments. Do not let us off with some generic prayer for "all people." They are your children as surely as we are; for them as for us Jesus Christ came into the world; he suffered and died; he was buried and was raised victorious over the powers that separate your children from you and from one another. So help us to pray carefully and thoughtfully for those sisters and brothers of ours whom we do not know and do not love and might not even like if we did know them:

> that brother of ours who is a stranger in our city, who came to this land of opportunity, who works and sends money home to a family whom he misses and for whom he weeps in lone-liness and prays in love;
> that sister who prays prayers different from ours, who may even call you by a different name, but who is your own sheep though not of this fold;
> those members of your human family in places where war and violence, ethnic and religious strife tear at the fabric of fami-lies, nations, humanity itself.

Remind us that it is for this world and these people that Jesus Christ lived and died and rose again: to show that your love embraces all the children of earth, and that we are all one in our needs, in our hopes, and in our reconciliation to you and to one another in Jesus Christ our Lord.

So we have let our requests be made known to you, O God, as the Apostle admonished us. Keep us, mold us, remake us day by day according to your desire and according to our particular need. When life batters us, bruises us, and sometimes baffles us, give us what we need to live faithfully and effectively: steadfastness, seren-ity, graciousness and good manners, balance and humor, gratitude and joy. And help us to treasure and to practice whatever is true, honorable, just, pure, lovely, gracious, excellent. Then let your peace that passes understanding keep our hearts and our minds in Christ Jesus, who taught us to pray . . .

Amen.

Thou Dost Beset Me Behind and Before

The psalmist declared:

O LORD, thou hast searched me and known me! . . .
Thou dost beset me behind and before,
   and layest thy hand upon me.

(Psalm 139:1, 5, RSV)

Let us come before the God who circumscribes our lives. Let us
pray: Eternal God, in majesty far above us, yet in mercy as near as
our particular needs, from whom to turn away is to walk in darkness, toward whom to turn is to dwell in the light, and in whom to
abide is to be held in steadfast love, we worship you this day.

In the security of your hold upon us, O God, we offer our prayers
of thanksgiving:

that we live not by chance within a random universe, but that
   our very existence is rooted and grounded in your intention;
that we are not made for ourselves or to be our own masters, but
   are called to live according to your purpose, in your service,
   and to the praise of your glory;
that we belong not to gods of our own making with whom we
   become so fascinated, and not to enterprises and causes, however noble, that would possess us, but to you — the origin,
   identity, and destiny of our souls, whom we would know as

23

we are known and love as we are loved of you in Jesus Christ our Lord.

We rejoice greatly:

in your love that called us into life and created us with the capacity to respond to you and to one another;

in your wisdom that from the deeps of your being calls to the deeps of our minds with the invitation to probe the wonders of creation and the mysteries of the heart;

in your providence that bears us up and sustains us in those times when our own strength of will and body and spirit are not enough;

in your grace that surprises and refreshes and renews us when we are dealing with more than we can face, more than we can bear, more than we can carry.

For these and countless other blessings that mark our life with you and form the overflow of your love for us, we give you our thanks and praise through Jesus Christ our Lord.

Within the embrace of your tender mercy we are able to see more clearly and to face more candidly all that is amiss in our lives because of our failure to live up to our birthright as your children. We acknowledge that our lives unfold under claims laid upon us by your sovereign love:

the command to do justice, to love mercy, to walk humbly with you;

the imperative to strengthen the faint-hearted, to support the weak, to serve you in ministries of compassion to the least of our sisters and brothers;

the requirement of stewardship from those to whom much has been given;

the obligation of open-hearted, open-handed generosity toward
the needs of others;
the duty of service.

When your love unfailingly secures our lives in Jesus Christ, gracious God, how can we not live as bearers of blessing, as heralds of hope, as the very body of Christ in this time and place? Reclaim us and renew us for faithful service in your kingdom, through Jesus Christ our Lord.

Within the faithfulness of your all-sufficient care, O God, we lift to you our intercessions on behalf of others. May those who seek for meaning, purpose, identity, belonging in lives that are without direction and peace know the joy of being found of you, of hearing you speak their names, of realizing that you have known them all along and have sought from the foundation of the world to welcome them into that place in your life that only they can fill. May those who mourn the death of a loved one know the comfort of your presence in their grief, and your promise of the triumph beyond tragedy in the fullness of your life and the faithfulness of your love, whence are all beginnings and whither is our destiny. May those who are afraid and who find courage failing, those who are lonely and long for community, those who are weary and who are ready to falter under their load find within the fellowship of your people — in this or some other community of faith — the encouragement, the comradeship, the comfort that are the very gifts of your Holy Spirit in and through the life of your church. Hear our prayers for peace where enmity begets violence and war, for good will where distrust and resentment sour the common life, for justice and righteousness where greed and selfishness have thrown life so far out of balance that the health of families and even communities is at risk, for compassion and generosity where cries from hearts beset by poverty and pain fall upon the ear of the wealthy and the powerful.

These and all our prayers we offer in the name of Jesus Christ our Lord, who taught us to pray . . .

Amen.

Grace to Help in Time of Need

In the Epistle to the Hebrews we read:

> As we have a great high priest . . . , Jesus, the Son of God, let us
> hold fast to our confession; for ours is no high priest who is unable
> to feel for us in our weakness, but one who has been tempted in
> every respect just as we are tempted, and yet did not sin. So let us
> approach the throne of grace with confidence, that we may receive
> mercy and find grace to help us in our time of need. (Heb. 4:14-16,
> author's translation)

Let us pray: At the beginning of another Lenten season, O God
our Father, we remember Christ contending with the tempter and
vanquishing him with a word:

> Begone, Satan! For it is written, "You shall worship the Lord your
> God and him only shall you serve." (Matt. 4:10, RSV)

Lest we lose our way upon our Lenten pilgrimage, we need the
guidance of your Spirit and the encouragement of your promise
that when we pass through the deep waters, or the dark night of
the soul, or the valley of the shadow of death, you will be with us.

Along this spiritual journey that will take us to the foot of the
cross and thence to the entrance to the empty tomb, give us wisdom
to look upward. Help us to understand that Christ's Passion and

death and burial were not merely events that you observed, but were events in which you participated . . . that in Christ you went through the agony of Gethsemane, through the God-forsakenness of Calvary, and into the dark abode of death . . . that his cross is your cross, that there is therefore no suffering, no hell of abandonment that you have not known and in which you are not with us to sustain and to keep us from falling.

Having lifted our eyes upward, O God, teach us also to look backward. We do not want to dwell in the past, but we would remember that this faith that keeps us . . . this story of your life with us . . . this Word that creates us and claims us and calls us into your kingdom's service . . . this gospel of the grace of the Lord Jesus Christ and the love of God and the fellowship of the Holy Spirit is radically historical. We would be reminded that Jesus Christ is not some spiritual ideal that we aspire to and strive for, but is your very personal, concrete engagement with us and with this world — that he is the defining reality of our life for time and for eternity.

Help us also to look outward. Remind us that the way of the cross, however personal, is not a private pilgrimage — that Christ said, "And I, if I be lifted up, will draw all people to myself." So open our hearts to our brothers and sisters. Make us instruments of your peace and compassion in the lives of those who are in pain or fear or despair, or in need of the ministry of our lives. As we have been beneficiaries of the faith, the grace, the influence of others, let our lives overflow in generosity, service, and open-hearted encouragement.

Help us to look deeply inward, that through the spiritual disciplines of worship and study, prayer and thought, we may be strong of faith to believe, strong of heart to love, strong of will to serve.

Finally, help us to look forward. There is much to do in the present time and in the places our lives are lived, O God, but remind us that where there is no vision the people perish. So let your Word enlighten and inspire us to live and serve and give of ourselves always with a vision of what is possible for those who hold fast to your promise, who listen for your call, and who follow bravely where your Spirit leads.

> Thou art the life by which alone we live,
> And all our substance and our strength receive;
> Sustain us by thy faith and by thy power,
> And give us strength in every trying hour. . . .

> Our hope is in no other save in thee;
> Our faith is built upon thy promise free;
> Lord, give us peace, and make us calm and sure,
> That in thy strength we evermore endure.
>
> (John Calvin, attr.,
> "I Greet Thee, Who My Sure Redeemer Art,"
> trans. Elizabeth Lee Smith, 1868, stanzas 3, 5)

Amen.

The Gift of Faith

An anonymous poet who understood the secret of faith wrote:

> I sought the Lord, and afterward I knew
> He moved my soul to seek him, seeking me;
> It was not I that found, O Savior true;
> No, I was found of thee.
> Thou didst reach forth thy hand and mine enfold;
> I walked and sank not on the storm-vexed sea;
> 'Twas not so much that I on thee took hold
> As thou, dear Lord, on me.
>
> (Anonymous, 1878, stanzas 1, 2)

Let us pray: Eternal God, we give thanks this day:

> that you have so made us that, in joy or sorrow, in health or
> sickness, in plenty or need we turn to you with the desire to
> pray that is itself the assurance that you have made room in
> your life for us;
> that prayer is our soul's response to your very being and presence
> and love touching our lives;
> that prayer, like faith, is a gift wrought and nurtured within us
> by your Spirit's seeking of us.

Just so, we ask you, O God, to help us believe more deeply and with greater understanding, and to pray more confidently and more thoughtfully, and more regularly. Some of us believe too easily and pray without giving much thought at all to how we conceive of you and what we ask of you. And so we pray for discernment and for guidance that, as we live with your Word and seek your will and contemplate the wonder of your love in Jesus Christ, our praying may reflect an ever more profound faith.

Some of us believe almost naturally and pray with deep conviction. We feel at home thinking about spiritual matters, talking about mysteries of faith, comfortable in offering prayer. And so we pray for humility and modesty lest we think of faith as an accomplishment rooted in our abilities rather than as a gift of your grace.

Some of us believe and pray only with difficulty, and only occasionally; and so we pray for the capacity to trust and to venture and even to risk doubting our doubts, lest we continue to gasp for spiritual breath rather than breathing deeply in faith.

Some of us hardly believe at all, and almost never pray, but want more than anything to know you and to have faith and to be able to pray. And so open us — our eyes and minds, our hearts and arms — to your spirit of truth, to your faithfulness and steadfast love. Grant us the strength to persist in our own quest for faith and understanding. Encourage us to see that, as hunger is a kind of testimony to the reality of food, so our wanting to have faith may become a strange kind of believing on the way to deeper trust and fuller confidence in Jesus Christ our Lord, in whom we see you face to face.

Hear now, O God, our prayers of intercession for those who most need our prayers, and for whom we are anxious to pray:

> a parent who has harmed a child through emotional, physical, spiritual abuse or neglect, or through the influence of a bad example upon this life of one who thinks a father or mother "walks on water";

31

children who live with a mixture of love and fear because of an
abusive parent;
parents who live with the heartache of a child's death, or illness,
or struggle with life;
persons who have never been loved or never known or believed
that they matter to anyone;
persons so alone they believe there is no one who will pray for
them;
those who do not, cannot, will not believe that you love them,
but only that you are angry, vindictive, and out to get them;
persons who are so broken and twisted by violence, anger,
self-loathing that they destroy every relationship they enter,
and every life they touch, including their own;
those who are deceitful and who do not honor truth or promises
or duties;
those who are trying to come to terms with the diagnosis of a
terminal, debilitating illness . . . who are coping courageously,
or barely, or who have virtually come undone; and those who
are their loved ones and caregivers;
those of us who know them and care for them and do not know
exactly what we should pray for.

We ask you to give strength, O God, to those for whom we pray
and who suffer from these evils. Make us alert to ways of touch-
ing their hearts and lives with the gospel of Christ. So often you
astonish us by granting requests that were only half formed . . . by
enriching our experience in unexpected ways . . . by reminding us of
factors we had overlooked. However you answer these our prayers,
may the outcome be that we love you more, that we understand your
purpose better, that we trust you and walk with you in greater confidence, through Jesus Christ our Lord, who taught us to pray . . .

Amen.

Our Maker and Keeper

LENT

One version of Psalm 100 reads:

Know that the LORD is God. It is he that made us, and we are his. (Psalm 100:3, NRSV)

Let us pray: Eternal God, because we did not make ourselves, because we do not keep ourselves, because we cannot forgive ourselves we reach out to you, our Creator, our Preserver, our Redeemer. We give thanks for the promise of your presence and strength when we have spiritual summits to climb, burdens to bear, temptations to resist, fears to overcome — in all those challenges, responsibilities, and duties that shape character, the facing and meeting of which help us grow into maturity of faith and life. Especially are we grateful for the providence under which our pilgrimage unfolds: the example of those whose faith and faithfulness are our legacy in Jesus Christ and as his church . . . signs of your sustaining presence often in unexpected persons and circumstances, reminding us of your promise that we do not walk alone . . . the irresistible evidence of Christian lives in which faith and hope and love abide and throw light upon our pathway. For all that surrounds us with your grace and in all that within us answers, we acclaim your goodness and speak your praise, through Jesus Christ our Lord.

We pray today, eternal God, for all who know you as the one in whom life and vocation are grounded, and who bless our community with the stewardship of their labors and the witness of their lives:

unpretentious saints and great-hearted sinners whose de-
meanor points beyond themselves to the grace that surrounds us all;

scientists and poets who explore the mystery of life, who let life
explore their minds and hearts, and who in formula and verse
set the mystery reverently before us;

teachers who, mindful of you as the author of truth and the mystery beyond all knowing, resist the temptation in themselves
and in their students to reduce truth to our limited capacities,
or to corner truth within our finite minds;

those who serve the law in the conviction that justice and mercy
partake of the Eternal, and who enact, enforce, and administer
law in that light;

those in business who shun the shoddy product, the inflated
price, the tyranny of the bottom line in an effort to serve the
public well, and to champion integrity in the common life;

physicians and nurses who seek the guidance and invoke the
spirit of the Great Physician in ministering to those who are
sick and in pain;

librarians who delight in making books available for the stimu-
lating of the mind and the feeding of the spirit;

police officers who serve and protect with firmness and
understanding;

those in the performing arts who awaken in us the good and
beautiful and true;

prison and hospital chaplains who quietly make their rounds day
after day in a ministry of hope and healing;

parents in crowded, blighted neighborhoods who defy their grim
surroundings and secure their children in a love that will not
quit.

Help them, and all of us, O God, to keep faith with our calling
and to keep faithfully at our labors, that through the ministries

of our lives, whatever they may be, our town may keep its soul, through Jesus Christ our Lord.

Now we pray for ourselves, O God, as Lent brings us near to the cross. Even as we mark Christ's Passion, we have a way of letting those very things master us that we should master in this season of self-examination and spiritual discipline. Help us to take those things in our lives that are very important — our work, our family duties, our community endeavors — and see them in the perspective of that which, in Jesus Christ, is all-important: your own decision to take our lives, with all their flaws and failures, into your own life, and to redeem us and all people. Help us to hear those words and claims that are illuminating and helpful: those good words that inspire and enrich our lives and deepen our understanding, and set them in relation to that Word that is incomparably and absolutely good and serious, comforting and wise in the fact that it is your own Word to us in Jesus Christ. Remind us that your Word is not merely an offer or an invitation to decide, but announces your decision concerning us, and that it is the Word we must obey in life and in death.

In the power of that living, active Word in Jesus Christ, O God, help us who pass through deep waters to trust your hold on us in the midst of the storm; reassure those who walk through the valley of the shadow of death that you are with them and will not let them go, and grant to those who watch and wait with them confidence that their loved ones are held in your everlasting arms. For those who ache with one they love beyond expression, or mourn for one who was their very life — a child, a spouse, a parent, a friend, a mentor — let them hear again the assurance that distress and death are included among "all those things" in which we are more than conquerors through Christ who loved us, and that cannot separate us from your love in Jesus Christ our Lord, in whose name we pray as he taught us . . .

Amen.

35

Blessed Is He Who Comes
in the Name of the Lord

In Luke's Gospel we read:

> As [Jesus] was now drawing near, at the descent of the Mount of
> Olives, the whole multitude of the disciples began to rejoice and
> praise God with a loud voice for all the mighty works that they
> had seen, saying, "Blessed is the King who comes in the name of
> the Lord! Peace in heaven and glory in the highest!" And some of
> the Pharisees in the multitude said to him, "Teacher, rebuke your
> disciples." [Jesus] answered, "I tell you, if these were silent, the very
> stones would cry out." (Luke 19:37-40, RSV)

Let us pray: Eternal God, we bring to you our prayers at the
beginning of this Holy Week when we follow our Lord Jesus Christ
into his Passion. As we remember his triumphal entry into Jerusalem, let our voices also sound his praise. Let our Hosannas greet
him who is our sure Redeemer, whose salvation reaches to the ends
of the earth, breaking down every barrier that would separate us
from you, enfolding in your mercy all creation such that were we
to keep silent, the very stones would cry out.

Ere the week is over, we will gather at Christ's table where, in the
Sacrament of bread and wine, he gives himself to us and gives us to
one another. Let his presence with us then and there, and the power
of his love, so fill our hearts with gratitude that we may answer the
gift of his life for our salvation with the gift of our lives in his service.

We remember Christ in Gethsemane; we mark his agony, his warfare of the soul, facing the cup of trembling set before him, draining it to the bitter dregs in the awesome mystery of your saving purpose. Incapable though we be of entering into Christ's agony, O God, help us to watch with him or, when we awake and hear the story again, to be given some marginal understanding of the love, the fear, the trust, the courage, the sacrifice set forth in such understated poignancy.

We will recall Christ's betrayal and note that when he spoke of it each of the disciples had to ask, "Lord, is it I?" And so do we. We will read that at his arrest, the disciples "forsook him and fled"; will we see ourselves fleeing among them? We will be spectators at his trial as the false accusations are brought by the princes of church and state, and as the crowds take up the cry: "Crucify him!" Were some of those the same voices that had sung "Hosanna!" only days earlier? Have we been that feeble in our own devotion?

We will hear the denial — thrice repeated — of the one closest to him of all the twelve. When, and in what circumstances, have our denials come, O God? Has it been when, like Simon Peter, to be identified with Christ might be dangerous? But for few if any of us has claiming Christ as Lord ever led to our arrest. No, our denials are more subtle and more insidious:

when we trivialize the gospel in the service of some selfish endeavor or lifestyle;

when we value Christ not for his truth that claims us, but for his usefulness to us in the pursuit of those things that really do matter for us — the personal and social and political causes in which we become so wrapped up;

when, in the name of inclusiveness, we acquiesce to the cultural pressure to relativize Christ and make him one of many doorways to truth;

when, in the name of orthodoxy, we use Christ as a club to compel conformity.

These are our denials and betrayals, O God. Beyond our guilt and shame, bless us as you did Simon Peter by restoring us to Christ's service, by believing that we do love him despite all evidence to the contrary, and by letting us hear those words of invitation: "Feed my sheep."

We will gather at the foot of the cross where, amid the scorn of the cynical and the cry of God-forsakenness and signs of cosmic crisis the Lord of glory goes to the mat with the powers of evil, sin, and death for us and for our salvation. And we shall know ourselves addressed and convicted in the rhetorical question of that old spiritual: "Were you there when they crucified my Lord?" Yes, we were there, O God, we are there . . . there where the powers of evil, sin, and death and their hold upon us are taken into your own triune life once and for all and forever. We were there, we are there, at that cross which towers over time as the supreme mark of your love for your children and your world. We were there, we are there, at that tomb in Joseph's garden where you were present in Christ's death even as you are present in our own.

Go with us, O God, day by day through this Holy Week, that in Christ's Passion we may see more clearly than ever before the proof of your amazing love . . . that "while we were yet sinners Christ died for us." These our prayers we offer in his name, and pray as he taught us . . .

Amen.

The New Covenant

Invitation to the Table and Prayer of Thanksgiving

The prophet Jeremiah spoke God's own words:

> Behold, the days are coming, says the LORD, when I will make a new covenant with the house of Israel and the house of Judah. . . . I will put my law within them, and I will write it upon their hearts; and I will be their God, and they shall be my people. (Jer. 31:31, 33b, RSV)

With the disciples at table on the night of his arrest, Jesus said:

> This cup is the new covenant in my blood. . . . Drink of it, all of you. (1 Cor. 11:25; Matt. 26:27, RSV)

Just so does God's word of promise summon us to this table. Just so does God's word made flesh meet us here in person. Just so are our lives "hidden with Christ in God" (Col. 3:3, NRSV) — taken into God's own triune life. In the bread and wine the covenant is demonstrated and renewed. We eat and drink to acknowledge that we do not live from or for ourselves alone. In Christ, God gives himself to us and gives us to one another, declaring to us in words that, Jeremiah tells us, are written on our hearts:

> I will be your God, and you shall be my people.

Let us pray: We come to your table, eternal God, with grateful hearts for the new covenant you have made with us in Jesus Christ, that you have sealed with Christ's blood, and that now and forever anchors our lives in your life. You have revealed yourself to us as Father, Son, and Holy Spirit, giving us to know that our Creator is our Redeemer, that our judge is our advocate, that our Lord is our Savior.

We give thanks that, because we belong to you, we belong to each other as children of the New Covenant. In Christ you have reconciled us to yourself and have called us to be reconciled one to another in him. So let us know in the depths of our minds and hearts, O God, that in Christ your love has truly broken down every barrier of sin and enmity that separates us from you, and from each other, and that at this table we are all children at home in the Father's house.

We are grateful that in Christ you have given us the ministry of reconciliation, and through us have elected to make your appeal in this community and in this world. So help us in our lives individually, and in our life together, to be profitable servants and winsome witnesses. Help us to set before our city, and to show forth to the world, the kind of living testimony of worship and service, of words and deeds, of thoughts and actions that reflects the Gospel's compelling authenticity, and that echoes its ring of truth.

Strengthen us anew through this Sacrament to witness a good confession in a world awash in trivial pursuits, and staggering toward spiritual dead ends. Let us not treat the gospel as mere human opinion, nor turn it into a tool of religious oppression; but let us share with joy and live with gladness this indescribable gift that is the light of the world and the hope of the world — your very life with us, for us, among us; and our life, each and every one, in you through Jesus Christ our Lord, who taught us to pray . . .

Amen.

40

For Us

Eternal God, as our Lenten journey draws to an end, we come in this final hour to the foot of the cross. In Jesus Christ crucified, dead, buried and descended, God-forsaken, into hell, we are brought trembling into the enacted reality of your reconciling love — your very self-surrender *for us!* In Christ you yourself become our salvation. You take into your own life the human condition: our brokenness, our mortality, our estrangement from you. You endure in the depth of your being the fullness of your own judgment upon the powers of evil, sin, and death that threaten to undo us. You bear them for us to the full extent of their power to hurt and destroy; and you bear them away.

As through Scripture and music we continue to meditate upon Jesus' Passion, cross, and death; and as in the silence of Holy Saturday we reflect on your own self-surrender for us, grant that we may be formed and guided, now and always, by the extent of your redeeming purpose, by the depth of your sovereign love, and by the triumph of your invincible grace revealed in this event that defines our life and death and destiny.

Let this knowledge direct the witness borne in our lives and the life of this congregation so that our words may be gracious, our judgments gentle, our actions generous; that our involvements may foster understanding and bring reconciliation in a divided world. So let us live that, through your guidance, we might be a blessing in our community in these days.

As we kneel in awe before the cross, O God, give us the assurance that our salvation is accomplished, completed, that in Jesus Christ you have thrown your very life around our lives and our life together. Give us to know that there is no life that your love has not reached, cannot reach; no circumstance into which your love will not enter; no brokenness of heart or health, hope, or trust in which your reconciliation and healing are not at work. Just so, separation from you can no longer be our destiny. In our self-will, in our desire to be the center of our own lives, we can and we do deny you, try to distance ourselves from you, seek to live by a kind of practical atheism as if there were no God who sees and cares and acts. But you have made it clear: the way that leads to our separation from you is now a dead end; that way is not open to us. In Jesus Christ you have walked that way in our stead, and no other footsteps cover yours there. That way you have mercifully closed forever.

Make us see, we pray, that our only prospect is surrender. We may doubt and deny and resist and renounce and ignore you, Lord God, but we cannot finally get away from the Love that will not let us go. However far and furiously we may seek to go from you, you will follow us, wait for us, watch over us, hold onto us . . . and you will continue to do so long after we shall have grown weary of our resistance. Your faithfulness toward us will be stronger than our doubt of you. In life and in death we belong to you, O God, and nothing in all creation will be able to separate us from your love in Jesus Christ our Lord, by whose life alone we live, and in whose name we pray.

Amen.

The Risen Lord

In his letter to the Philippians, Paul employs the words of an early Christological hymn, saying of Christ that "though he was in the form of God, [he] did not count equality with God a thing to be grasped, but emptied himself, taking the form of a servant. . . . And being found in human form he humbled himself and became obedient unto death, even death on a cross" (Phil. 2:6-8, RSV).

Let us pray: Eternal God, as the heavens are high above the earth, so are your thoughts higher than our thoughts. And yet you have reached across the gulf between eternity and time, between the infinity of your vast domain and the particular places where we live and move and have our being within the boundaries of birth and death. You have covered every distance we have created to keep you away, broken down every barrier we have erected against you. In Jesus Christ you have lived our life and died our death, the Son bearing in himself the burden of our denials, our rebellions, our continuing, tragic determination to be our own gods, removing our transgressions as far from us as east is from west, breaking the hold upon us of the powers of evil, sin, and death, and accomplishing our salvation. So did the Apostle Paul continue in that early hymn:

> Therefore God has highly exalted him and bestowed on him the name which is above every name, that at the name of Jesus every knee should bow, in heaven and on earth and under the earth, and

every tongue confess that Jesus Christ is Lord, to the glory of God the Father. (Phil. 2:9-11, RSV)

So does Christ tower even now above earth and time: the sovereign Lord who suffered, lifted upon his cross to draw all people to himself . . . the risen Lord who reigns in the power of the love that will not let us go . . . the living Lord, present in the power of the Spirit to chasten and challenge, to wound and heal, to break down and build up, to judge and to reconcile until the kingdom of this world has become the kingdom of our Lord and of his Christ, and he shall reign forever and ever.

And so we pray, O God, let Jesus Christ be the peace of our world, and his vision guide us in shaping our life together. May his righteousness lead us in the way of justice, fair dealing, and good will. May his compassion inspire us to gentle judgments, kind gestures, encouraging words, and merciful actions. May his faithfulness inspire in us a devotion to tell the truth, to keep our word, to honor our commitments. May his promise to be with us always strengthen women and men in times of trial and trouble, in sickness and suffering, in disappointment and despair, in heartbreak and grief. May his steadfast love for us, even unto death, both remind us of the length to which you have gone to reconcile us to yourself, and inspire us, in his name, to take up the ministry of reconciliation he has given to us.

Thus it is, O God, within the awesome and defining drama of Christ's emptying himself to accomplish your redeeming purpose that we know we must work through the implications and demands placed upon us by this choice you have made and this thing you have done in Jesus Christ. We know that you are at work in us intentionally and persistently to make use of the stewardship of our lives in bringing about your purposes in the lifetime and place in which your providence has established us. Help us then to open ourselves and our life as a congregation to the working of your Spirit in and among us, that we may serve and not stifle your work in this place, and that we may help and not hinder any who would come to you, believe in you, love you and serve you through Jesus Christ our Lord, who taught us to pray . . .

Amen.

God's Purpose in Us

In his letter to the Ephesians, Paul declared:

For we are [God's] workmanship. . . . (Eph. 2:10, RSV)

Let us pray: Eternal God, from whom we come, for whom we were created, to whom we are accountable, and by whom our lives are set within your purpose and held in your providence, we worship you this day. We come with grateful hearts, and with the prayer that by your Holy Spirit we may serve you with grateful lives.

Help us, O God, to be women and men and young people of deeper, stronger, and growing faith. Help us to remember that we belong to you and that nothing can separate us from your love in Jesus Christ our Lord. So help us then to trust you in all things: in success and disappointment, in gladness and in grief, in health and in sickness, in hope and in fear. Work with us, O God, we pray; teach us and open our eyes until we see, in the life we live, in the commonplace circumstances that fill our nights and days, in the creative possibilities of the human mind and spirit, in the mercy within human relationships, and even in the desert places of life, something of the powerful grace and providence that form the nurturing context of our being in you, and of your purpose in us. Perhaps then shall we know how to bend the knee in prayer, and how to sing your praise in spirit and in truth.

Help us, O God, to be people of grateful obedience. Remind

us that your intention undergirds our very lives, and that we were created not for aimless wandering or for trivial pursuits, but to live to your purpose and glory. So open us to discern more readily your particular purpose for each of us. Show us how our special talents and abilities, when exercised with a sense of call and stewardship, may become spiritual assets in the service of the gospel. Show us how a prayer offered, a stand taken, a word spoken, an hour volunteered, or a vote cast on behalf of justice and compassion can become a building block in the kingdom of God. Teach us never to underestimate the influence in the economy of your kingdom of a single Christian life, however unspectacular or unnoticed it may appear. Rather, remind us of the potential of precisely that life in yoke with Jesus Christ who is able to do anything, and who strengthens us for all things.

Help us, O God, to be bearers in the world of Christ's own mercy and forgiveness. As those who have been forgiven much, help us to forgive. Help us to keep always before us the cross of Christ as a reminder that you have taken the sins of the world upon and into your very life, and there have judged them and broken their power. So enable us to take this liberating word to those who continue in bondage to a beaten enemy, those who have not heard of their deliverance. Help us to bear that word and to demonstrate that word in our relationships with them. We pray particularly for those who have not understood that they belong to you and not to self . . .

or to that habit or that addiction or that prejudice;
or that dark, mean, judgmental, hateful, resentful spirit;
or that self-righteous, self-centered approach to life and relationships.

Help us to know that because Jesus Christ lived and died and has been raised from death, our first and last word to the world is a word of grace and life, of forgiveness and mercy, of possibility and promise . . . and that if we would rather speak condemnation in Christ's name we should perhaps just remain silent altogether.

Remind us, O God, that there is no way to deal with the imperfections of life, no way to keep the human spirit from despair, no way to bring peace to the soul, no way to realize your purpose in us save through forgiveness, faith, obedience, and worship — into all of which Christ gathers us and forms us as his people, teaching us to pray as he taught his disciples . . .

Amen.

Praying with the Bible

The psalmist wrote:

> Your word is a lamp to my feet
> and a light to my path. (Psalm 119:105, NRSV)

Let us pray: Eternal God, far above us in majesty and mystery, yet near to us in the eagerness of your love, we worship you this day.

We lift our eyes to the heavens and are awestruck at the wonder and immensity of the universe, so that the psalmist's question is ours as well: "What are we mortals that you are mindful of us?" We lower our eyes to regard the locale of our own lives and relationships, our accomplishments and failures, our hopes and fears, our time of being that runs its course and comes to an end; and we join with the psalmist in calling you "our dwelling place in all generations." Let it not be, O God, that we remain uncertain of your presence and your care, but grant that we also may sing with confident trust:

> Thou dost beset me behind and before,
> and layest thy hand upon me. . . .
> Whither shall I go from thy Spirit?
> Or whither shall I flee from thy presence?
> If I ascend to heaven, thou art there!
> If I make my bed in Sheol, thou art there! (Psalm 139:5-8, RSV)

49

O Lord, do truly and powerfully beset us behind and before. Come into the secret chambers of our souls where we never let anyone in and make your home there. Sift through all that has accumulated there; remove and cast out what is mean and selfish and hard-hearted, and establish and enliven "whatever is true, whatever is honorable . . . just . . . pure . . . lovely . . . gracious and compassionate and kind"; through Jesus Christ our Lord.

Come to us, O God, and lay your hand upon us at the point of our deepest need. Some of us are troubled in soul and pray to you out of depths of discouragement that only you can reach, and from which only your powerful promise can deliver us to hope. Help us to hear Christ's words as his personal assurance to us: "Let not your hearts be troubled; neither let them be afraid."

Some of us come to you with joyful gratitude and vigorous enthusiasm for life that is filled with blessings: a family life tender with love and warm with devotion; friendships that undergird and encourage, ministering to our best life; work and service that ask of us our best and bring us a sense of satisfaction and the knowledge that we are appreciated. There are possibilities, opportunities, responsibilities that allow us to live toward a future of promise and hope in this good and prosperous land. We thank you, O God, for every benediction of life that lifts our hearts and fills our souls with rejoicing. Let us not hoard or squander, dishonor or profane such blessings. Let us not be tempted to say: "My own hand has gotten me this bounty." Rather, let us hear the Apostle say to us, "What have you that you did not receive?" And so make us such trustworthy stewards of each and every blessing that we may not look ruefully on gifts wasted, opportunities missed, hopes that were so much greater than the harvest of life. Rather, may we hear our Master's approbation: "Well done, good and faithful servant; enter thou into the joy of thy Lord."

Some of us come to you tired. Although our commitments have not changed, we do not seem to have the energy we once had.

Strengthen us if it be your will; but if not, let us be of help and of service to those who need our encouragement, that the word to your servant Job may come to describe us:

Behold, you have instructed many, and you have strengthened the weak hands. Your words have upheld him who was stumbling, and you have made firm the feeble knees. (Job 4:3-4, RSV)

Some of us come to you ill and afraid. Help us to fear most of all a loss of confidence that we can do all things through Christ who strengthens us; and for the rest, O God, remind us of your promise:

When you pass through the waters, I will be with you. (Isa. 43:2, NRSV)

Some of us come to you heartbroken, O God, for one has died who, because we loved them so, was life itself to us. Stand close to us, we pray, in our grief — so close that we may feel your everlasting arms around us to hold and to uphold. Let us know your presence beside us unto and into and beyond that death that still fills our hearts with quaking and our minds with doubt. And then let us take comfort in our grief that, in accord with Christ's promise to us all, the one whom we love now beyond the limit of sight is at home in the Father's house of many rooms.

And some of us come to you, O God, who are strong. Could it be that this means you have work for us to do, and are calling us to take up challenges and to step forth to lead by example? Consecrate us and our energies for the causes of your kingdom and the service of your world and your children. Help us to give our minds to know the truth, our hearts to love the truth, and our wills to do the truth that is in order to goodness.

We offer our prayers for good will among the nations, for a sense of responsibility to the common weal among those who shape public opinion, for a renewed commitment to bringing thoughtfully, winsomely, and wisely a God-consciousness, a Christ-perspective, a faith dimension to the public square. Give us wisdom, courage, strength of will and body, determination that we may serve you in ways that prepare the way for the day when the nations "shall beat their swords into plowshares, and study war no more" . . . the day when "they shall not hurt or destroy in all [your] holy mountain" . . . when "the earth shall be full of the knowledge of the glory of the LORD as the waters cover the sea."

These and all our prayers we offer in the name of Jesus Christ our Lord, who taught us to pray . . .

Amen.

Prayers for the Children of God

See what love the Father has given us, that we should be called children of God. And so we are. (1 John 3:1, RSV)

Let us pray: Eternal God, with love beyond our imagining, beyond all deserving, and sometimes beyond our belief, you have set your heart upon us and called us your children. And so we are . . . gathered again at this table where we are fully known, and where your love in its full expression is set before us. Some of us have known all our lives that we belong to you. Some of us have never known it, and still cannot believe it — such knowledge is too wonderful for us, such love too good to be true. Some of us have come back to the table from wandering in some spiritual, or emotional, or moral far country. Help us to understand that, however we have come, it is a love stronger than any estrangement that has drawn us here, and that welcomes us home.

As children of God we give thanks that yours is a love that seeks us and does not require that we make the first move, that while we were yet sinners Christ died for us. As children of God we confess that too often we live as if this defining fact of our lives does not matter greatly. We deny Christ with our lips and with our lives; we make choices and take actions as if there were no God who sees and cares, much less one to whom we belong and to whom we are accountable. Forgive us, O God, the practical atheism in the ways that we deny you and betray our own birthright, and restore us to the place at your table prepared for us from before the foundation of the world.

As children of God we marvel that you are able to work your purposes in us and through us. As much as we want to be successful and effective in the enterprises of your kingdom, we know that we will not always be so . . . that we may well not very often be so. And yet you have done, and you still do work your will in and through our failures. So help us, above all, to strive to be faithful that, whether in success or failure, we may find the meaning of life in your service, and commit the outcome of life to your sovereign judgment and omnipotent grace.

As children of God we pray now for the witness of the church: in every local congregation, may worship be offered reverently and faithfully, faith be deepened and strengthened, and ministry bring healing and hope. And in the church universal, O God, may the gospel be so clearly proclaimed and compellingly demonstrated that people will come from east and west and north and south to sit at table . . . and to see what love the Father has given us that we should be called children of God . . . and so we are, through Jesus Christ our Lord, who taught us to pray . . .

Amen.

Risen, Ascended, Reigning

A verse of Matthew Bridges' great hymn calls us to prayer on this
Ascension Sunday:

> Crown him the Lord of life, who triumphed o'er the grave,
> And rose victorious in the strife for those he came to save.
> His glories now we sing, who died and rose on high,
> Who died eternal life to bring, and lives that death may die.
>
> (Matthew Bridges,
> "Crown Him with Many Crowns," 1851)

Let us pray: Eternal God, you rule over all that you have made.
Your sovereignty is revealed in the steadfastness of your love, in
the constancy of your righteousness, and in the faithfulness of your
mercy. In the story that unfolds upon the pages of the Bible, we learn
of your ruling, accompanying, redeeming of all life, of each life, of
our life. You created the world to be the stage upon which the drama
of salvation unfolds. It tells us who you are, and reminds us that we
belong to you. It announces your blessing to all the families of the
earth. It promises your own presence with us to save and to bless, to
claim and to command, to judge and to correct, to reconcile and to
redeem. This drama reveals a God "merciful and gracious, slow to
anger and abounding in steadfast love," a God who, like a mother,
cannot forget her infant, a God who, like a father, runs to welcome
the lost one home, because the name of each of us is graven on

the palms of your hands and etched upon your heart. All of your promises, in the fullness of time, come to fulfillment in Jesus Christ your Son. Could it really be, O God, that this Jesus who was born in a cattle shed and cradled in a manger . . . who announced and incarnated in our midst your very rule of grace . . . who was arrested, convicted, and crucified under Pontius Pilate — could he really be, as this strange and wondrous story claims, the one in whom the entire meaning of life and history and the universe is revealed?

Is he truly the risen Christ, ruling at your right hand as King of kings and Lord of lords? Is this story truly our story, O God? And if it is, as you say it is, then we need a very different perspective upon life if we are going to live in and by this story. We are so ensnared by the affairs of our daily lives, our frantic attempts to manage things and control people and make circumstances work to our purposes. We traffic in what can be seen and touched and handled, evaluated and used. We take our cue from what the headlines report about the movers and shakers, about presidents and premiers and prime ministers, about market forces and power brokers. We even try to use Christ and you, O God, to gain advantage or to justify our desires and decisions. We need a perspective that allows us to discern your hidden presence. We need to listen above the noise and blare to what you would say to us, because they are words that only you can speak. We need to look beneath the glamor and beyond the superficial and behind the spectacular and see what remains hidden — what eye hath not seen:

your very presence hidden in an infant wrapped in swaddling clothes;
your victory over the powers of evil, sin, and death hidden in that same one as he dies upon the cross;
your vindication of faithfulness, compassionate service, and steadfast love as the ruling reality and the secret of life in the commonwealth of Christ the King in whose name we pray.

So grant, O God, that we might find in Christ's rule:

courage to bear his name and to follow his way of righteousness
and compassion and mercy in the world;
determination to live our lives and give our energy to those
things that make for peace, that promote good will, and that
bring about reconciliation among all families of the earth;
strength when the load of life threatens to break us;
reassurance, when we are ill and afraid, that our King is also the
Great Physician;
comfort, when our way leads through the valley of the shadow
of death, that our King is the Good Shepherd.

Draw near to all who are in special need of your strength and
care, O God, and in your ruling, accompanying, redeeming presence may they find the sure and steadfast anchor of the soul, praying
always in Christ's name, and as he taught us . . .

Amen.

The Fruit of the Spirit

Eternal God, on this Day of Pentecost we come before you with joy and gratitude for the gift of your presence in your world and in our lives by your Holy Spirit. Creation itself testifies to your readiness, before the foundation of the world, to be God not in isolation, but in relationship. From the beginning you spoke to your creatures and you heard their cries. Your very name is your promise of your presence with us: "I am who I will be . . . I am the One who will be there with you and for you." In Jesus Christ your word of promise became flesh and dwelt among us — Emmanuel, God with us. Before his death Jesus promised his disciples that you would send the Holy Spirit to be with them forever. The risen Christ promised his presence with us always. At Pentecost your Spirit spoke clearly and compellingly to the gathered multitude "from every nation under heaven," and has since empowered, directed, and corrected your church in every generation according to your word.

Hear our prayer this day, Lord God, for the continued presence of your Spirit to guard and guide us as we seek to serve you in these days. Remind us that life in the Spirit looks upward and outward far more than it looks inward, and that the Christian life is, above all, gracious and grace-filled, and not a harsh, burdensome, hard-nosed legalism. Grant that our lives and our life together might bring forth an abundant harvest of those fruits of the Spirit that point to the rule of grace that is the kingdom of God in the world.

Help us, O God, to bear the first fruit of the Spirit: love — the "more excellent way" that leads us out of self-centeredness and self-absorption into engagements marked by generosity and relationships grounded in a spirit of graciousness. By this foremost spiritual gift, deliver us from jealousy and boastfulness, arrogance and rudeness, ill-temper and resentment into a determined good will ready to "bear all things, believe all things, hope all things, endure all things" and to remain steadfast in faith and friendship against whatever life throws up before us.

Create in us, we pray, the fruit of joy — the un-summoned welling up of gladness that fills the heart, that delights in your goodness and grace, and in the good and gracious things that happen to us, undeserved, in the working out of your providence — that this joy may flow from our lives into the lives of others in a wider harvest.

Make us people of peace, O God, peace that is more than the mere absence of conflict or the lessening of anxiety, but that upholding sense of serenity, even in stressful times and hostile circumstances. Grant us that poise and inward calm that comes from unfaltering trust in your care and safekeeping. And by your Spirit of peace make us instruments of your peace wherever and among those of your children to whom you direct our lives.

May our lives bear also the fruit of kindness. Create in us, O God, a comfortable and comforting temperament that others may find us easy to be with, talk with, work with, relax with. So may we reflect your own kindness that leads, the Apostle tells us, to repentance and faith, and forms lives of gratitude and obedience.

Inspire in us, gracious God, the fruit of generosity, a true character of benevolence and a settled disposition to have a mind and heart and will for the good, the needs, the well-being of others.

Encourage in us the Spirit's fruit of faithfulness in the keeping of our word, in standing by our commitments, and in holding fast to what is good even when to do so is difficult and costly.

Grant, Lord God, that our lives personally and our life together might yield a harvest of the fruits of gentleness and self-control. In our vocations, in the various projects and undertakings that need our abilities and claim our commitments, kindle in us the desire to do well what needs doing, but with the least degree of self-assertion possible in order to be effective, that our example may be more winsome than overbearing, it being the Spirit's way to beckon rather than bludgeon, to lead rather than to drive. So help us to be able to lose ourselves in the service of those things that build up the communities of faith and life to which we belong, and that help to make and keep human life truly human.

So may it be, O God, that as we walk in the Spirit and live by the Spirit we shall become living witnesses to the mind and heart of Jesus Christ in and through lives of unselfconscious love and service, and in so living become more truly and fully ourselves — our own actual best selves in accord with your designs for us all, through the grace of the Lord Jesus Christ, the love of God, and the communion of the Holy Spirit.

Amen.

The Faithfulness of God

The psalmist declared:

As the mountains are round about Jerusalem,
so the LORD is round about his people. (Psalm 125:2, RSV)

Let us pray to the Lord who encompasses our life: Eternal God, the psalmist's poetry speaks to us of your enfolding of our life so that we know ourselves aright only as we understand that we are dependent upon you for life, bound to you as the Lord of life, answerable to you for the stewardship of life, destined for you in and beyond life.

There are times when this knowledge takes hold of us in the depth of our being and we are glad, grateful, filled with what the psalmist called "the joy of your salvation." At other times we feel alone, as if we belong to no one, as if no one cares about us one way or another, as if our lives are of little worth, without much meaning, unappreciated, and to no lasting purpose.

Whence comes this sense of aloneness? These feelings of discomfort, O God? Are they sent to us from somewhere beyond? Do you send them upon us from time to time? Or do we, by the way we live and the choices we make and the decisions we take, wander into their emotional territory?

The mountains about Jerusalem spoke to the psalmist of the permanence, the faithfulness, the steadfastness of your love — not of

61

the waxing and waning of your care and presence. In the thunder of rushing waters, said another psalmist, something deep in you calls constantly to the depths of our souls — the persistent, patient, perpetual press of your Being upon our consciousness, your Word upon our heart, your Life upon our life. Your people spoke of a covenant of love and promise into which you draw us to yourself and draft us into your service. No, dear God, we cannot claim that your desire for us is merely occasional, your determination to make good your claim upon us only episodic, that you are of two minds toward us. Jesus Christ is your mind toward us — toward all people. Jesus is not "yes and no," but in him all of your promises find their Yes — their fulfillment.

And so, O God, the sense that we are alone and without purpose that all of us feel some of the time, and that some of us feel much of the time, is due, we confess, not to your having turned away or given us up, but to our living, deciding, acting as if we belong not to you but to ourselves . . . as if our own wills and desires, our own purposes and expectations are sovereign. Thus do we learn, merciful God, that the sins of pride, self-sovereignty, self-will, self-indulgence are finally also self-defeating. Thus do we learn that your holiness will simply not indulge our denials . . . that you have determined to reconcile us to yourself, not to reconcile yourself to us, so that it is we who must conform to your pattern for our life in Jesus Christ, and not you who must prove acceptable and useful to us.

The good news in all of this that fills us with gladness is that you are not willing to leave us in despair — that you know about us what we have chosen to deny: that we are yours, and that in Jesus Christ you have so united your life with ours that nothing will be able to take us from your hand or separate us from your love.

So break through our denials, our discouragements, our despair and remind us that life itself and each of our lives centers on you and your purposes:

purposes that graciously and mercifully include us and draw us
into your heart;
purposes that call us to lives of compassion, justice, and righteousness in our relationships one with another and toward
those upon whom life bears down especially hard;
purposes that would adorn our lives and our life together with
truth and grace, kindness and trustworthiness, peace and
good will among and between peoples and nations;
purposes that would undergird commerce with honesty, friendships with faithfulness, homes with gentleness, human hearts
with high purpose and good faith in every undertaking.

On this Memorial Day weekend, a time in our nation's life for
recalling those on whose shoulders we stand, whose labors have
blessed us, whose gifts are our legacy, we would remember especially those whose sacrifices have secured the good life in the good
land that we enjoy:

parents whose gifts to us are more than we can number;
teachers who believed in us and called forth from us our best;
artists who inspire us;
inventors who astonish us;
crusaders for justice and compassion who challenge us to vision
and action on behalf of those in need;
pioneers who go before us and lead us;
prophets who remind us that we are yours and are accountable
to you for the stewardship of our own lives;
soldiers:
. . . heroes proved in liberating strife,
who more than self their country loved,
and mercy more than life.
(Katherine Lee Bates,
"O Beautiful for Spacious Skies," 1893, stanza 3)

Chiefly we would remember Jesus Christ: his reconciling life, his atoning death, his victorious resurrection, his continuing power to save and redeem.

So strengthen and encourage us, O God, in every good work to realize your sovereign intention for us, in us, and through us. And continue to press upon us, and to disturb and correct us with your judgments so that, whether we are confident or confounded at any particular time, we know you as the encompassing presence of our lives — as our Creator and Lord, as our judge and redeemer, through Jesus Christ our Lord, who taught us to pray . . .

Amen.

We Believe; Help Our Unbelief

In the letter to the Hebrews we read:

> For whoever would draw near to God must believe that he exists,
> and that he rewards those who seek him. (Heb. 11:6b, RSV)

Let us pray: Eternal God, we would draw near in faith and in
our seeking be rewarded by your finding us. You are too myste-
rious to be explained, yet too near to be ignored. You transcend
our thoughts, our imaginations, our words, yet in no place either
physical, emotional, or spiritual into which we may wander aim-
lessly or betake ourselves willfully can we escape you. Not only do
you know us and name us, but in Jesus Christ you have come to
us in person and have declared something irrevocable about your
intention toward us and for us, and about our place in your purpose
and in your very life.

Not that life with you is an easy matter, O God. Often it is with
us, as Jacob discovered, more a striving, a wrestling, a grappling.
We have our doubts. Help us to be honest about our doubts —
honest enough to express them to you, and honest enough also to
consider that you yourself may well be behind the questions that
disturb us, leading us by doubt, through doubt, beyond doubt to
a stronger, more thoughtful, and hard-won faith. Thus do you
enable us to grow in spirit and in truth toward deeper understanding, more reverent worship, more faithful obedience to the

great commandment that we love you with heart, soul, mind, and strength.

Just and righteous God, when we are tempted to withdraw from the struggle with complex issues of personal morality, and with the ethical imperatives of social justice and righteousness, be patient with us, but keep the pressure on us until we understand that it is your Spirit who struggles in us and with us to teach us that faith must always seek understanding, and that to trust in your care is, even at some cost, to obey your call. Remind us that even after his resurrection Christ bore the scars of crucifixion that marked his life with us. So also, our life with you may leave us wounded, limping along the way of faith, but ere we let you go, you will have blessed us, and made us to be a blessing.

We offer our intercessions to you, O God, on behalf of a world that is in danger of war and violence and destruction. We need your wisdom as nations face one another at the brink of conflict, or as movements seek ways to kill and frighten in what is sometimes a desperate desire for justice, and at other times an insatiable lust for power and revenge. Bring wisdom and sound thinking, a vision of justice and righteousness and good will to the leaders of our own nation and other nations: that they may understand the ultimate futility and failure of war; that those who shape public opinion and who lead armed forces and who create international policies of nation with nation may be motivated not by fear and frustration, but by an undaunted determination to learn peace, to govern with justice, and to work together in a spirit of compassion and good will, and in the service of life and not death.

Eternal and all-gracious God, from whom every family in heaven and on earth is named, whose care for us is reflected in a father's compassion and a mother's comfort, and whose love is more constant and enduring than that of any father or mother, we thank you for the openness to the wonder and mystery of faith nurtured in us by parents and grandparents in our infancy, our childhood, and our youth. We thank you for the faithfulness they demonstrated and their consistent intercessions on our behalf across the years that, even when we were unaware, have been anchors to our souls. We thank you for sisters and brothers, teachers and colleagues and friends whose belief in us, and whose example, have encouraged us along our way. In your providence, O God, they have shaped and guided, blessed and upheld us in our pilgrimage of faith. As you have been the God of our forebears, our families, our churches, continue in these days to hold us among your people so that our children, and our children's children, may live in the wonder of your gospel.

When our minds wander from your way, O God, and our hearts rebel against your claim, turn us back to yourself. It is in the fullness of your grace and truth that our thoughts and affections have their true home. Help us to find in you the waiting father who welcomes us with open arms and great rejoicing. So then we will be able to pray out of that faith that is your gift, your reward, your blessing:

> Let me no more my comfort draw
> From my frail hold of thee.
> In this alone rejoice with awe:
> Thy mighty grasp of me.
> (John Campbell Shairp, "In His Hands," 1819–1885, stanza 3)

These and all our prayers we offer in the name of Jesus Christ, your Son, our Lord, and we pray as he taught us . . .

Amen.

Prayers for the Common Life

Jesus said:

> If you abide in me, and my words abide in you, ask whatever you will, and it shall be done for you. . . . You did not choose me, but I chose you and appointed you that you should go and bear fruit and that your fruit should abide; so that whatever you ask the Father in my name, he may give it to you. (John 15:7, 16, RSV)

Let us therefore come confidently to God in prayer: Eternal God, in Jesus Christ you have come to us and taken us into your life, into your heart, into your kingdom's workings in the days of our lives. Christ himself both taught us to pray and encouraged us to pray in his name. And so today we join our prayers to the great chorus of prayer that sounds from your church at all times, and in all places where the gospel has taken hold of the human heart.

We give thanks that you are, and for the fullness and mystery of your being as Father, Son, and Holy Spirit. We are grateful for what it means that you are the Creator, the Lord, the Redeemer of the universe and of all who dwell therein. We thank you most of all for Jesus Christ our Lord in whom we know you as God with us, whose character is love, whose kingdom is the sovereign rule of grace in and over all of life. We are grateful for his love that seeks us in our wandering, saves us from our folly, sets our lives within your purpose, and strengthens us for the opportunities and responsibilities, the demands and duties to which you call us.

Help us, O God, to be faithful citizens, serving you in the common life. Help us to stand, to speak, and to work for good government. May we learn to nurture a public spirit that respects human dignity and is sensitive to human need, and that challenges the attitude that politics must always be divisive and contentious. Teach us how to encourage public policies and government programs in education and community development that treasure the potential of young minds, encourage human endeavor, and nurture the human spirit.

We pray for the public life of our nation. Guide those elected to govern to know the difference between public service and personal ambition, to honor the public trust above private gain and political calculation. May those in government and industry, in labor and commerce, whose decisions affect the lives of countless women and men and families never forget the human factor and faces that lie within the numbers and statistics, margins and bottom lines that so easily drive policy decisions.

We pray for sisters and brothers whose lives are lived out under tyranny — where the common lot is oppression, cruelty, fear. Help them to know that they are not forgotten in the greater human family, that their plight is lifted to you in prayer by people like us who do not even know their names, but who know that you call them by name. Grant that we may never ignore or dismiss their deprivation in the security of our freedom, and grant that the light of liberty that glows in this and other lands may keep alive in their spirits the hope of liberation that is the promise of your kingdom.

We pray for ourselves and for others in the exercise of personal decisions and self-discipline. Temper our desires that we may not make choices that bring harm to others, or that violate the preciousness of life or love. By your Spirit within and among us bind up broken hearts, broken spirits, broken relationships.

Hear our prayers of intercession:

for those whose hearts are restless, that in you they may find true
rest and confidence;
for those whose homes are unsteady, that they may bring their
need to your tender care, and their decisions to your guiding
wisdom, and find in you a firm foundation against forces that
would break hearts and destroy sacred ties that bind and bless;
for those whose health is breaking, that they may be strengthened by your healing presence;
for those whose hopes are fading as life refuses to measure up
to their plans and expectations, that they may not overlook
blessings that are abundant in life to those who have eyes to
see.

Because it is crucially important whose lead we follow, O God,
help us to give over to you the direction of our own lives. And grant
that as a church family we may strengthen one another through
burdens shared, through joys marked in common, through mutual
encouragement of words exchanged, prayers offered, friendships
nurtured, and work undertaken in the name and spirit of Jesus
Christ who binds our lives to your life, who knits our hearts in a
common faith and hope and love, and who taught us to pray . . .

Amen.

The Proper Place of Fear

The book of Proverbs reminds us that

The fear of the LORD is the beginning of wisdom. (Prov. 9:10, RSV)

Let us pray: We utter such words, eternal God, and find ourselves straightaway in the presence of infinite mysteries, mighty contradictions, towering interrogations, overwhelming revelations. Words from beyond us sound in the midst of life's flowing stream:

In the beginning God created the heavens and the earth. The earth was without form and void, and darkness was upon the face of the deep. . . . And God said, "Let there be light"; and there was light. . . . So God created humankind in his [own] image . . . ; male and female he created them. (Gen. 1:1-3, RSV; Gen. 1:27, NRSV)

The years will pass as a tale that is told, and our maps of the universe will change a bit, but you, O God, will be forever; and at the end of all time you will judge the earth and all that you have made. Creation and consummation, dim beginnings and distant end, the unfolding design of providence, birth and death, body and soul — thus is the pattern of your purpose woven in and around our lives, in vast and solemn mysteries of agony and ecstasy, of hopes we can hardly express, of opportunities that demand our best efforts, and blessings that redeem our shortcomings and failures.

You move in on us, Lord God, the Beyond in the midst of life. In the revelation of yourself you bring down the walls we erect to define ourselves and to protect the selves and lives we have constructed. You lift us out of our isolation and leave us standing before the awesome breadth and length and depth and height of being. You show us the hell and the heaven of common circumstances and consequences of life. You tear the veil from the face of time and reveal the splendor of eternity. "The Spirit searches the deep things of God," wrote the Apostle. No wonder we draw back, hold back from this word, this presence that opens and lays us bare before your eyes.

And yet, O God, in much of your searching out of us you are not always so daunting. Sometimes you move quietly but irresistibly to sweep the anxieties and ambitions and reputations of our preferred order of things into oblivion before our very eyes. The things we labor so frantically to possess, and now grasp so tightly and competently, fall by their own weight when the word from beyond us again falls on our ears: "This night thy soul shall be required of thee." So many frantic years, so many anxious nights, so many bargains struck and tricks played, so many little advantages sought, so many limited goals met, so much ambition for such brief possession. That word comes again: "A person's life does not consist in the abundance of possessions."

Why then, O God, do we continue to grasp for and lean on all the props that earth affords? We hold on to money, but its value ebbs from day to day, so that yesterday's sufficiency is tomorrow's bare necessity. We look to pleasure, but it soon turns to the flat taste of despair. We straighten our shoulders, lift our chins, and count on ourselves. But how presumptuous for such changeable creatures: a mixture of good and evil, saint and sinner, victims of freedom torn by incompatible desires, with awful doubts and shining faith. Who shall deliver us from this human quandary?

No wonder we try to busy ourselves with less disturbing matters than your presence in our lives, O God. Are we afraid of what you might do to us? Afraid that if we open the door of our souls you will seize control of our wills without our consent or desire? We want to keep our hands on the reins, to have the say-so regarding our lives, to be sovereign in our freedom, to turn this way or that as we choose, to dabble and play, to follow the way we prefer to go whether that way leads anywhere or not. Your power and presence and purpose, O God, are overwhelming: you created the universe; you uphold it; you will judge and redeem it. We fear that if your power really got hold of us it might be the end of us . . . and yet . . . who knows? It may be the beginning of a new creation.

We remember, gracious God, that in Jesus' parable of the Prodigal Son, after the boy had lost everything from his home to his inheritance to his honor, the story says, "He came to himself." It takes a great deal to reveal ourselves to ourselves — so many things get between our eyes and our souls. It may be wealth, ambition, comfort — none of them essentially evil, but nevertheless obstructing our sight so that we never see clearly that we are souls made for Another, and restless apart from that essential belonging. In Jesus' parable, when the boy came to himself, vulnerable in all his needs and shame and despair, he said poignantly and significantly: "I will arise and go to my father." And the father, who had let him go away, but who had never let him go, ran to meet him. So may we run eagerly, O God our Father, into your eternal embrace in Jesus Christ our Lord, who taught us to pray . . .

Amen.

Let Us Worship God

Calling God's people to worship, the psalmist says:

> Enter his gates with thanksgiving,
> and his courts with praise!
> Give thanks to [the Lord], bless his name! (Psalm 100:4, RSV)

Let us pray: Eternal God, our Maker and Master, your steadfast love endures forever, and your faithfulness to all generations. We come before you with praise and gratitude:

> for your goodness that called the world into being and fashioned women and men to live for the praise of your glory;
>
> for your Word that engages us, reminding us that we belong to you, claiming us anew in every need and circumstance, directing us in your way as "a lamp to our feet and a light to our pathway";
>
> for your mercy that forgives the sins whereby we deny you, betray your commands, wreck our lives, and abuse our souls;
>
> for your grace that ministers to us through the countless mysteries of your providence, and draws us patiently by countless pathways and relationships into abundant life;
>
> for your presence at the beginning and end of life, and your companionship through all the transition points and breaking places of life: able in all things to keep us from falling,

assuring us that even when life reaches its depths, we are not alone, your Spirit bearing witness with our spirits that we are children of God, through Jesus Christ our Lord.

Bless us, O God, that in your presence our thoughts may be clarified, our hearts thrown open, our spirits lifted to fuller life and finer service.

Give to those who are perplexed the light of truth and understanding. Let forgiveness lift and heal the guilt of those who break under its weight. Let peace take hold of the hearts of those who are torn inwardly by conflicting desires and who know not where to turn. Bring comfort to those who suffer pain, a calming spirit to those who are anxious, and renewed energy to those who are tired but who must carry on ere they lay their burdens down. Bless those who are insecure, and even afraid, in the face of life's deepening mysteries. Give them the confident assurance that you are within and beyond all mysteries and all knowledge as sovereign, faithful, and loving Lord. By your present Spirit, strengthen and encourage those who are in difficult circumstances, hemmed in by pressures and responsibilities that never seem to let up. Draw near in an intimate way to those who are alone, that in knowing you close to them their days may be brighter and their nights less lonely. Walk beside those whose work and duties place them in danger, that your mercy may guard them from hurt and harm. Stand with all of us, O God, that we may bear the responsibilities life demands of us — whether these be heavy or modest — with faithfulness, patience, compassion, and grace, through Jesus Christ our Lord.

And now, eternal God, we pray that you would give shape to our lives in accord with your purpose. When life is hard and our way leads through difficult decisions, give us courage. When the way we should go is not clear and we do not know what to do, give us insight and guide our thoughts and actions. When we fail you and others and ourselves, forgive us, restore us, and hold us lest we fall farther from your way. Then, by your guiding hand, let us return to your way for us, and in your Light let us see light that we may understand ourselves better and be more confident in your claim upon us. So shall we follow with less hesitation, and walk with less stumbling toward and into that spiritual depth and stature that is your high purpose for our lives, and your promise to us in Jesus Christ our Lord, who taught us to pray . . .

Amen.

For Those at Life's Breaking Places

Through the prophet of the Exile, God's people in Babylon heard their Lord speak to them in words of hope and salvation:

> Do not fear, for I have redeemed you;
>   I have called you by name, you are mine.
> When you pass through the waters, I will be with you;
>   and through the rivers, they shall not overwhelm you;
> when you walk through fire you shall not be burned,
>   and the flame shall not consume you.
> For I am the LORD your God,
>   the Holy One of Israel, your Savior. (Isa. 43:1-3, NRSV)

Let us pray: Eternal God, whose providence and grace always reach far enough to cover our waywardness and our wandering, we give thanks that you have picked up the broken pieces of our past, and promised us a future secure in your presence and within your purpose. Make us grateful and faithful stewards of the present — this gift of life and time in which to work out our salvation with reverence, trust, and obedience. This, O God, even as you work in and among us to accomplish your good pleasure, and to make us instruments of your kingdom's ends. May that same providence and grace be to us the continuing source of confidence and courage as we go through the breaking places of life.

As we consider times of great change and adjustment to life's demands, O God, some of these are happening to us and they occasion prayers of petition for ourselves. Others, that we can only imagine, involve people we know and love and care for, and so become the burden of our intercessions. We call you Father, and we liken your tender care to that of a mother. Hear us as we pray for:

children who are going off to school: little ones to kindergarten, excited, anxious, perhaps a little weepy, almost as much as mother and father are;

older children taking the daunting step into middle school or high school — passages to new challenges and adjustments . . . physical, emotional, academic, social . . . as they move from childhood into adolescence and toward maturity;

young women and men entering college with the even more stringent demands of classroom and campus that call for mature decisions and the exercise of self-discipline and self-control and self-direction . . . aware, or perhaps unaware, of how constantly they are brought to you in prayer by loving, proud, grateful, anxious parents and mentors.

Faithful God, we know you as One who makes and keeps covenant with your children. Hear our prayer for those who are just beginning life together as husband and wife, having sealed their covenant with vows, that their love and appreciation for one another may deepen and grow stronger within your gift of marriage.

You, O God, are the Creator and Giver of life. Hear our prayer for parents preparing to welcome a first child or another child into their lives that they may receive this child as a blessing, and may in turn be a blessing to their son or daughter.

God of mercy, hear our prayer for husbands and wives going on with life after the death of a spouse who was life itself to them: grant that their love may be sanctified in sacred memory, and that they will know sustaining companionship within the circles of family, faith, and friendship.

God of all comfort, hear our prayer for those parents who have lived, they know not how, through the death of a child — that they may know you near to them in a powerful way as their God who bears with them the pain of their grief, and who sustains them. Hold them close until they are able to lift their heads again in the strength of your own suffering in Jesus Christ, and your promise that, in his victory, death's sting will not prevail over us or our loved ones.

You call us, O God, to new paths of life and service. Hear our prayer for those who are newcomers to our city or neighborhood, having left their homes elsewhere to make a home among us. May they find in this community and, if in your providence it be so, in this congregation a warm and gracious welcome in the name of Jesus Christ. We pray for those beginning a new job, that they may find their abilities wanted, their efforts valued, their talents appreciated, their gifts needed and nurtured, and their souls nourished in a community of mutuality and good will. Guide us, O God, in and through and past life's various breaking places where they must be faced. Sanctify our memory of that which is past, but not lost; enable us to know forgiveness for that which is best left behind; and grant us to live in the present with courage and confidence that we and all whom we love belong to you and that, wherever life calls us to be, we are held in your steadfast and redeeming love, in Jesus Christ our Lord, who taught us to pray . . .

Amen.

Chosen before the Foundation of the World

Paul opens his letter to the Ephesians on a note of gratitude to the God and Father of our Lord Jesus Christ who, before the foundation of the world, chose us and destined us in love to be his children through Jesus Christ. It is a moving testimony to the Christian conviction that our lives have their origin and destiny in God.

Let us pray: Gracious God, you have created us for yourself and claimed us as your own. In Jesus Christ you have linked your life to ours, and you continue to work your saving purpose in us, with us, for us, among us. On this day of confirmation we give thanks that life and faith have their origin, their unfolding, and their fulfillment in you, and we claim anew Christ's promise to be with us to the close of the age.

We give thanks for these young women and men who today, by profession, confirm the faith in which they have been nurtured. We are grateful for their lives . . . for the preciousness of each one, for the possibilities that lie before them, for the promise of blessing to others that resides in the abilities and talents that have been given them in your providence.

We give grateful thanks for parents who have loved them, encouraged them, and nurtured them in homes where your presence was acknowledged, your name honored, your will sought as guide and strength. We remember with gratitude vows taken at the font in the Sacrament of Baptism . . . vows to surround our children with our love, to cherish their lives, to encourage their growth in faith, and to challenge them to open their lives to Christ's call and leading.

Having heard these young Christians make their professions of faith, O God, we give thanks for those who have been their teachers in this place from their infancy to this day, and those who have worked with them over the months of their preparation for this day: for those who have told them the stories of the faith within the larger story of your life with your people and your world . . . for those who have listened to them and talked with them about what it means to believe in Jesus Christ as Lord and Savior, to be a member of Christ's church and to live as Christ's disciple in this world.

On this day of their confirmation we pray that these young women and men will continue to grow in the faith they profess. Grant that they may be faithful to the best they know and believe. Help them to be willing to ask questions — even difficult questions — as their faith intersects with life and its demands. Grant that they may keep faith with those who have gone before them in the Christian way and on whose shoulders all of us stand as we seek to be faithful in our own day. Help them to remain open to the leading of your Spirit toward new insights into and new perspectives on the gospel of the Christ who is your living Word, and who, as he promised, goes before us into every tomorrow, and remains with us at the edge of every moment. Grant them to grow in faith, through doubt, toward and into deeper understanding. Help them always to respect the faith of others and to bear their witness faithfully, with confidence in you and your Christ, and in the spirit of him whom you sent to the world you loved, not to condemn but to redeem. As their faith is tested and as they wrestle with the difficult demands of faith and life, help them to remember your promise to those whom you have created and redeemed:

When you pass through the waters, I will be with you;
and through the rivers, they shall not overwhelm you;

when you walk through fire you shall not be burned,
and the flame shall not consume you.
For I am the LORD your God,
the Holy One of Israel, your Savior. (Isa. 43:2-3, NRSV)

And now, O God, grant us as a congregation to join with these confirmands in rededicating ourselves to the faith we have tried to keep and that has kept us across the years of our lives. Help us all, in our life together and in our lives personally, to be instruments of your righteousness and justice, agents of your peace and reconciliation, that in our time and in all that we do we may serve your redeeming purpose for the world, in Jesus Christ our Lord, who taught us to pray . . .

Amen.

My People Whom I Formed and Made

Through the prophet of the Exile God reassures his captive people in Babylon, calling them sons and daughters,

> . . . whom I created for my glory, whom I formed and made. (Isa. 43:7, RSV)

Let us pray: Almighty God, as we come to you in prayer, we acknowledge the majesty of your power and wisdom, the persistence of your righteousness and justice, the expanse of your love and command. We come, not because you need anything from us, but because you have made us for yourself . . . you have made yourself known in relationship to us . . . and except we pray we deny our very identity as your children.

We cannot fail to praise you from whom all blessings flow, for you have breathed into us the breath of life, placed us in your good creation, and commanded us to lift our voices in praise.

We cannot fail to confess before you our failure to live in your light and to follow in the way you have set for us, for your mercy lifts us when we fall, and your love blesses and bears us along our way.

We dare not fail to bring you our grateful thanksgiving, for your providence sustains us, your righteousness challenges us, and your justice guides us.

And so we lift our hearts to you that they might again find in you their true home, and that in your Spirit our spirits might be encouraged and made strong for the duties and responsibilities to which you call us in Jesus Christ our Lord.

Continue, O God, to form us as your people in this place, and structure us, individually and as a congregation, for faithful living and effective service in your name. We need your help: in sorting out thoughts and situations about which we are confused; in arranging priorities that are out of order; in clarifying our understanding of what is important and necessary and right, to which we must give ourselves; and what is not so important that it could not be set aside for now.

We need for you to strengthen wills that have grown soft and unaccustomed to disciplined obedience. Where we have been damaged and hurt, we need for you to bind up our broken and wounded spirits, that in your strength we may be strong to forgive, and be able for the duties of life.

We want to make a difference for Jesus Christ and for his kingdom, and for the way of life to which he calls us. So give us, we pray, bigger, kinder, more understanding hearts . . . ears more sensitive to cries for help . . . clearer eyes of faith to see where Christ, going before us as he promised, calls us to follow and to feed his sheep.

And now, O God, give focus and shape to our intercessions that we may remember in prayer, and neither forget nor forsake, those who are ill or anxious, alone or afraid, heartbroken or discouraged. Help us to see whom we may help, and be eager to go to them in your name.

As a new school year opens in our community and in our church, hear our prayers for those who are teachers and mentors . . . those who try to nurture in our children and youth a love of learning, a desire for knowledge, a devotion to truth, a growing faith. Encourage them in honoring the life of the mind to be teachers and not just testers. Help those who nurture the faith of our children to teach by loving example and with the spirit of Christ. And give us the wisdom to encourage our teachers, to support them, and to appreciate them in the high calling they often follow at great personal sacrifice. Give us as a community, and as a community of faith, a renewed respect for our teachers, and the will to give them what is necessary to keep faith with their calling and with our children.

Gracious God, you have formed us and made us. Continue to refine the work of your hands, we pray, that as servants we might be profitable in the work of your kingdom, and as your children bring you honor, through Jesus Christ our Lord, who taught us to pray . . .

Amen.

Be Not Afraid

Like a litany of encouragement, God's reassuring word runs through Old Testament and New:

Fear not, for I am with you, be not dismayed, for I am your God. (Isa. 41:10, RSV)

Let us pray: Eternal God, we have heard what you have said and still say to your people in Scripture, and how your Spirit speaks to our hearts and souls. Now we must talk with you about our fears and uncertainties and anxieties for the world, and for our nation, and for ourselves in these days. We bring to you our fears for our families, our loved ones, our children, our jobs, our financial resources, our abilities to meet whatever the days will demand of us and from us. We are even a little bit afraid, O God, that we will think only of ourselves and of those people and things we call our own, and that we might shut out of the circle of our concern people who need us and whom we might help and encourage and reassure. Fear has a way of doing that to us — of turning us in on ourselves and away from others. Help us, we pray, to trust your promise to hold us up, and to hold us together, and to hold us close. Give us confidence by the nearness of your Spirit, and do not let us lock ourselves up in a fortress of fear.

We pray for all whom darkness and despair threaten to overwhelm; those in the depths of pain and grief; those bewildered or depressed; those on whom the burdens of responsibility and decision weigh heavily and unrelentingly: our president, our secretary of state and other cabinet members, the commanders and soldiers of our nation's armed forces. As they, in petition, pray for your guidance, may our petitions echo their own, and our intercessions hold them steadily before your throne of grace.

We pray that all who are going through a time of trouble may be given the confidence and serenity that are the gifts of your Spirit; and that the knowledge of your presence and love may bring a dawning hope even to those who feel that all is lost.

Hear our prayer for all who are anxious and afraid, all who are impoverished by falling values; all who feel that the worthwhile things are crumbling away. Show us new gleams of hope and opportunities for good, and make our caring for one another's needs one of the ways that faith takes hold of us, and hope takes root in us. Let the helping hand of human sympathy and compassion and hospitality hold up the stumbling and give fresh courage to the frightened.

It is you, O God, who have taught us to pray like this. If it were not for the revolution in attitudes which you have brought about through Jesus Christ, we should not have these ideas about involvement and reaching out to others in love and good will. Christ commanded us to love God with all our being, and to love our neighbor as ourselves. Lord of the two great commandments, what are we to do? How are we to love? We need your further help to turn good ideas into action and behavior. May your church never give up saying what it knows to be your will about the place of other people in each person's life. May Christian communities in all places exhibit a spirit of sharing, a sensitivity to human need, and a willingness to reach out in response to this need.

Few of us, O God, are people of great influence and responsibility, and we wonder how our prayers can affect the course of the world's life. We cannot believe that war or tyranny or famine or sickness are conditions under which you intend people to live. And yet many have prayed for peace, but war has not been averted. The terrorists will fall only after they have caused much misery. We believe that terrorism and the wanton murder we have known are evils to be fought, and yet we know that humanity itself is not equipped to fight them. We need the strength of will and the power of love that only you can give — love which is prepared for great sacrifice, creative thought, and untiring patience. Meanwhile, we ask you to give strength to all who suffer from these evils and to make us alert to ways of making justice, compassion, and peace real and lasting in our world.

We pray for our country that none may exploit others, and none be neglected or forgotten; that we may be quick to reward service and to recognize true worth and pressing need; and that all may work for the common life and welfare.

We pray for the life of the world: that every nation may seek the way that leads to peace; that human rights and freedom may be everywhere respected; and that the world's resources may be ungrudgingly shared.

We pray for the communities to which we belong, that we may be good citizens. Make us willing to accept responsibility when we are called to it, and able for every opportunity to speak, to stand, to act for righteousness, justice, and peace. Grant that our influence may be wholesome and not harmful, good and not evil.

We pray for the generation to which we belong, those in all nations with whom we share a common fund of memory, common standards of behavior, and a common attitude toward and vision for the world. Grant that the presence of Christ may be so real to us that we may be able to help our generation to see him also as our contemporary.

O God, into whose world we come and from whose world finally we must go: we thank you for all those people, great and humble, who have maintained the fabric of the world's life in the past and left us a great inheritance. May we take up and encourage what is good, and hand it on to those who come after, believing that our work in your name will not be in vain.

God our Father, as we look upon the world and see the evil and suffering in it, we easily doubt your goodness and your purpose. Help us to move beyond our doubts to deeper faith. There is much of which we cannot be certain, and yet in Jesus Christ we see enough to know that you love us. Because of what you have done in Jesus Christ we know that in spite of all that is wrong in this world, it is still your world. Help us all to accept your purpose and, as we consider Jesus Christ, to see by faith that nothing — no suffering, no evil — can finally frustrate your will, or separate us from your love. By faith, O God, we see your purpose for our nation. May our life as a people be more and more an expression of your love. Give us a greater compassion for the homeless, the unemployed, and all in need of the community's help.

We thank you, O God, that with the gift of your Son you provide for us so much else — an example to live by; an anchor of hope in the midst of darkness and storm; the spirit of love; the promise of life. We pray that all over the world Christ's church may possess these gifts in abundance and may bestow them willingly upon others. Where evil forces rob women and men of justice and humanity, give insight and realism and endless compassion to all who seek to end the power of those forces. Where habits of violence rob women and men of reason and mercy, keep alive in our leaders a vision and sense of responsibility that will spur them to deal with causes as well as with symptoms. And where accident or deliberate injury, hatred, or cruelty bring pain and terror and long seasons of distress, may your love keep reaching out in the hands and voices of those who tend and who soothe and who cure, so that even in the valley of the deepest shadow there is never lacking a life-saving light from heaven.

Lord God, in all these things you see the whole where we see only the part. We call upon your wisdom and your love. We enfold within the arms of prayer all whom we have named in our hearts this day, whether they be present to us or absent from us, and all whose need is great. May the day come when pain shall be banished, illness conquered, violence ended, terrorism destroyed, and evil itself done away. Father, keep us now and to all eternity, in the fellowship of those who would seek and know and love and do your will.

Lord, you so often astonish us by granting requests that were only half-formed in our prayers, by enriching our experience in unexpected ways, by reminding us of factors we had overlooked. In whatever way you answer these prayers, may the outcome be that we love you more deeply, understand your purpose more fully, and believe in you with greater confidence and trust. It is Jesus Christ who prompts us to form these prayers; it is in his name that we offer them, and we pray as he taught us . . .

Amen.

This prayer was offered shortly after September 11, 2001, and includes phrases and ideas adapted and arranged from several prayers in the section titled "Further Prayers for the Life of the World" from *A Call to Prayer: Public Worship through the Christian Year,* edited by Caryl M. Micklem (Grand Rapids: Wm. B. Eerdmans Publishing Co., 1993). The prayer intended to acknowledge the grief, anger, and fear in the hearts and minds of the worshipers, while also claiming the assurance of God's sovereign presence and guidance as we were sorting out what our Lord and our faith demanded of us in such circumstances. In this instance, our congregation's worship was fed and our lives blessed from the treasury of Christian prayers in Micklem's valuable collection.

World Communion Sunday

Jesus said:

People will come from east and west, from north and south, and will eat in the kingdom of God. (Luke 13:29, NRSV)

Let us pray: The words of our communion hymn still echo through the sanctuary, O Lord Christ:

Just as I am, thy love unknown
Has broken every barrier down;
Now to be thine, yea, thine alone,
O Lamb of God, I come, I come.
(Charlotte Elliott, "Just As I Am, Without One Plea," 1836, stanza 6)

Here at this table we take the bread and wine remembering that in your Passion and death you gave yourself to us and gave us to each other. Is this the place, O Lord, where we see most clearly the reality of the church as your body . . . the body of Christ . . . and ourselves all as members of it? All of us here today, yes, but on this day millions of people of every race and tongue, every nation and clan, every fellowship and tradition of worship within Christendom come at your invitation to be remembered into your death and into your life. There are no barriers left to prevent it, O Christ, for your cross has removed them all: our sin you have borne and broken;

the power of evil you have confronted and defeated; death, the final enemy, you have engaged and overcome. The barriers of denial, unbelief, rebellion, self-will that we erect are no match for the love that will not let us go, even when we are hardly worth holding on to. Your mercy is greater than our waywardness, your faithfulness toward us stronger than our doubt of you. Our only option is surrender. Thus do we come to your table with grateful hearts and voices raised in thanksgiving, praying as you taught us . . .

Amen.

The Word of God

In the beginning was the Word, and the Word was with God, and
the Word was God. (John 1:1, RSV)

God speaks, and we are able, in prayer, to answer.

Let us pray: Eternal God, our prayers are less our reaching to
find you than our grateful acknowledgment that you have found us
and have bidden us to pray. Straightaway, then, we pray in thanksgiving for your Word that establishes us as your people. We are
grateful that you commanded the world to be . . . and it was so;
that your Word came to us in the Law and the Prophets. You command us to worship you alone, and to love you with all our heart
and soul and mind and strength. You teach us how to live toward
one another and in your world with righteousness and justice as
people for whom you are God. You call us to account, judging and
correcting us when self-will undermines our trust and turns obedience to rebellion. You restore, reconcile, and redeem us for that
life with you for which you created us, and to which you continue,
by your Holy Spirit, to shape and form us. Most of all we give
thanks for your Word incarnate in Jesus Christ who dwelt among
us, full of grace and truth, and who links our lives to your life for
time and for eternity.

Grant, eternal God, that we might not receive your Word care-
lessly or with indifference. Help us rather to expect your Word, to
listen for it in Scripture and in the proclamation of the gospel, and

to give your Word a receptive hearing amid the other words and voices that bid so persistently for our loyalty. Amid the tensions and enmities in our world and in our nation, let your words shape the words of our mouths and the thoughts of our hearts. Let your Word continue to claim us, to bind us to yourself, and to conscript our abilities and employ our energies to serve the tasks of your kingdom. Help us to believe that the promises and commands and challenges contained in your Word are for us, and that we can trust your Word as a lamp to our feet and a light to our pathway. Let your Word, living and active, sharper than any two-edged sword, lay our lives open to you, O God; that in your penetrating, wounding knowledge of us we may come to know the depth of your mercy, and the power of your healing love.

Then, make us eager to take your Word to others and grant that our witness may be full of grace, clarity, and good will. So may it be that in knowing you as the One with whom we all have to do, those who hear the gospel from our lips, and read it in our lives, and see it in our works, may be assured of your love for them, your promise to them, and your presence with them in Jesus Christ our Lord, who taught us to pray . . .

Amen.

Thou Restoreth My Soul

In his need for God the psalmist cried out:

> O God, you are my God, I seek you,
>   my soul thirsts for you; . . .
> as in a dry and weary land where there is no water.
>
> (Psalm 63:1, NRSV)

Let us pray: Eternal God, so far above us that we cannot comprehend you, yet so close to us that we cannot escape you, we come to worship and to be renewed. We confess that life itself . . . and our own life . . . depends upon you. We acknowledge that you have made the human soul to correspond to you, and that to be without you is to be like a thirsty creature beside a dry riverbed, confused and desperate.

Sometimes we feel that way, O God. Some of us feel that way today, and we pray that you would restore our souls. We may not really understand what it is that causes the gnawing dissatisfaction, the sense that something is not right with our lives, especially when we obviously have so much for which to be grateful. Is it because we have let certain things in life come between ourselves and you and cause us to forget that we are made for you and belong to you? If trouble at work or at home, anxiety about our own or our family's or our children's future, another person's hostility, financial setbacks, sickness, danger, death seem to be consuming our thoughts, then restore our souls. Remind us again that none of these things has separated us from your love, because none of them can do that . . . that in all we are called upon to face, now or at some time or another, you are with us as you promised: to uphold, to sustain, and to guide. Remind us that in all these things we belong to you, and not to them or to their power to hurt and destroy. So seek us out in the special need or circumstance that is given us to face: young or old, glad or grieving, rich with friends or desperately lonely, healthy or frail of body. And restore our souls lest good fortune make us think we do not need you, and lest ill fortune make us think you have forsaken us.

If need be, O God, restore our souls by being stern with us about the demands for righteousness and justice, about the grateful benevolence and service that are attendant upon being your people and enjoying the benefits of your providence. Deliver us from ethical carelessness, from moral laziness, and from every kind of self-indulgence. Keep us from deceiving ourselves or making exceptions of ourselves regarding those commitments of heart and disciplines of will that must shape our lives and our life together as your people. As those to whom much has been given . . . and much forgiven . . . help us to be generous and merciful in the way we deal with people, whether intimate friends, frequent associates, or casual acquaintances. Teach us to welcome opportunities to show compassion and offer a helping hand to others. Let your Holy Spirit shape our overall stewardship of the blessings entrusted to us and the mission committed to us in Jesus Christ our Lord.

A soul restored, O God, is a soul with concerns far beyond itself, and so we bring you now our prayers of intercession on behalf of others. We pray for peace among the nations, and commit to your care and encouragement those who work for peace and understanding in our world — elected leaders, dedicated citizens, peace keepers and peace makers and peaceful spirits — that their vision and their efforts may bring wisdom and good will to fruition in a harvest of justice and compassion. We pray for those who protect us by risking their own lives: those in military service and those who guard us at home. Keep them, we pray, in your care.

We pray for your church in the world, O God, a great company of your people who bear witness to Jesus Christ and to the gospel in every land and nation. In her need, sustain her; in her weakness, strengthen her; where she is persecuted, deliver her; where she is faithful, encourage her. Help us in this congregation always to be grateful for the sisters and brothers to whom we are bound in the fellowship of Christ's body. Help us to pray for them and to remember that they pray for us. We know there are those who call us enemies and who pray not for us but against us. We pray for them today, as difficult as it is to do so, because you have told us, in Jesus Christ, to pray for our enemies and to overcome evil with good. Help us to know how to pray appropriately for our enemies, and how to hate what is evil without being vindictive and embracing evil ourselves. Make us as a congregation loyal in our life and mission, our worship and witness. To members and ministers alike give vision, wisdom, devotion, generosity, and big-heartedness that we may reflect the spirit of Christ in our life together, and be his faithful servants in and for the life of this city.

Having come to you in need, O God, let us go out with our souls restored and our strength renewed in Jesus Christ our Lord, and in the power of his might, the One who taught us to pray . . .

Amen.

A Mighty Fortress Is Our God

God is our refuge and strength, a very present help in trouble.

(Psalm 46:1, RSV)

Let us pray: Eternal God, we sing the great battle hymn of Martin Luther, "A Mighty Fortress Is Our God," on this Reformation Sunday and are ourselves drawn into the confident faith and powerful confession of Psalm 46, which inspired it. Here we join our hearts and voices to the liturgical and prophetic expressions of devotion and trust that arose in ancient times from your people at worship and from prophets of your word, and that reverberate now in the inner chambers of our hearts and the deep reaches of our need. Like them, we are confident not in our own strength — that would be futile indeed. Rather, we are confident because of your promise to be with your people across the ages and, in the fullness of time, to be with us and with all people in person, your promise faithfully fulfilled in Jesus Christ our Lord.

So center our thoughts in prayer not around our strength, but around your power and your presence. Help us to know you as our refuge from physical danger — as the shepherd who knows your sheep by name; as the Great Physician who heals our brokenness; as the stronghold of our lives against our own self-destructive choices and self-defeating sin.

Merciful God, grant us to know you as our refuge when life tumbles in upon us — when the psalmist's imagery of the earth changing, the ocean depths rumbling, the waters roaring, the mountains trembling seems to describe what is happening in our hearts and minds as we watch jobs end abruptly, marriages fail, families break apart, children live in fear, and loved ones fall ill, and as we are called to walk through the valley of the shadow of death with parents, spouses, and children. In such times, O God, throw your strength around our need and hold us secure in the embrace of your love.

Faithful God, grant us to know you as our refuge against those forces that tear at the fabric of society. When narrow vision and fear of those who are different tempt us to look and to live only within the circle of self-interest, widen our outlook, stretch our minds, open our hearts, enlarge our concerns for community and country and the commonwealth of nations that we may work to build a world of justice and understanding, of respect and cooperation, of generosity and good will. When nation rises up against nation by violence and terrorism, show us again the self-defeating nature of war: that it brings destruction to those who practice it; that those who would by violence subject history to their power will be wise to regard the ruins of nations and empires that forgot that one power alone is exalted over the earth — that you alone are God whose work it is to make wars cease, to break the bow and shatter the spear and destroy the tools of violence, and whose help is the refuge of those who call upon your name.

Grant us to know you, O God, as our refuge against all that assaults our souls. When greed lures us, make us generous. When pride would make us pompous, make us instead gracious. When envy bids to control us, help us to rejoice in the blessings of others. When we begin to turn in upon ourselves, give us instead a spirit of gratitude and a heart for friendship. When we are tempted to sloth and indifference before the great challenges of life, give us a sense of obligation, of duty, of stewardship in the employment of the gifts that your providence has assigned to us as resources in the service of your kingdom.

And when we are tempted, even in your name and in the service of quite noble causes, to presume to tell everybody else what to think, and how to vote, and what to believe, and how to behave, and what they have to do to be judged faithful to you, then give us a strong measure of humility that allows us to acknowledge what is so obvious, and yet so difficult for us at times: that you are God, and we are not. Help us to heed the words you have spoken to us through the psalmist: "Be still, and know that I am God." Through Jesus Christ our Lord.

Amen.

A Great Cloud of Witnesses

For all the saints who from their labors rest,
Who thee by faith before the world confessed,
Thy name, O Jesus, be forever blest.
Alleluia! Alleluia!

> (William Walsham How,
> "For All the Saints," 1864, stanza 1)

Let us pray: We gather at Christ's table on this Sunday of All Saints, eternal God, with grateful hearts for the great company among whom we are numbered in this communion.

We give thanks that it was with this in mind that you created the world — to be the stage upon which the drama of salvation was to unfold. We give thanks that in our Lord Jesus Christ all of your promises find their fulfillment:

your promise to Abraham that your call to him would issue in the blessing of all the families of the earth;
your promise to Moses to be with and for and among your people to save and to bless, to guide and to discipline, to correct and to redeem for your name's sake;
your promises to David and to Isaiah and to Jeremiah that there would come one who would be the Savior of the world, the prince of peace, the servant-Messiah who would be wounded for our transgressions and bruised for our iniquities, the one

who would initiate a new covenant and who would draw people from east and west, from north and south to sit at table in the kingdom of God.

As surely as you are faithful, eternal God, Jesus Christ is not "yes and no," but in him all of your promises find their "yes."

And so we gather today in thanksgiving at the table where his words sound again: "This is my body given for you . . . This cup is the new covenant in my blood." We are mindful that with us here in the communion of saints are many faces and names we hold in sacred memory:

parents who gave us life and faith, love and encouragement;
teachers who helped us to grow in understanding and in wisdom;
mentors who did and who still do model for us what the Christian life looks like;
friends and loved ones who, in death, we have only recently handed back to you;
men and women who have defined "church" for us and for whose lives and witness we continue to be grateful.

As we look around us, we are mindful of and grateful for those whose faith and sacrifice literally built this church, women and men whom many of us never knew, but who bless us through their legacy.

Thou wast their rock, their fortress, and their might;
Thou, Lord, their Captain in the well-fought fight;
Thou, in the darkness drear, their one true Light.
Alleluia! Alleluia!

(How, stanza 2)

Since we are surrounded by so great a cloud of witnesses, grant, O God, that we may run with perseverance the race that is set before us, faithful in our day to you, and to those on whose shoulders we stand in faith and in life.

> O blest communion, fellowship divine!
> We feebly struggle, they in glory shine;
> Yet all are one in thee, for all are thine.
> Alleluia! Alleluia!

(How, stanza 3)

Amen.

On Holding Things Together

Paul wrote to the Colossians:

[Christ] is before all things, and in him all things hold together. (Col. 1:17, RSV)

Let us pray: Eternal God, ruler of creation, Lord of history, Father of our souls whose hand holds us and guides us in accord with your purpose, we worship you this day and give thanks for all those whose talent and calling it is to hold things together.

Most of all we are grateful for Jesus Christ, your Son, our Lord.

He is the image of the invisible God, the firstborn of all creation; for in him all things in heaven and on earth were created. . . . He himself is before all things, and in him all things hold together. (Col. 1:15-17, NRSV)

Gracious God, we give thanks as well, and we pray for those women and men who, in your providence, have been given the ability to unify, to reconcile, and to hold together people and enterprises and efforts to high purpose . . . those who bring a welcome perspective, competence, grace, and stability to all their endeavors:

public servants, who hold together opposing political agendas and so make government work for the common good;

business and community leaders who are people of vision, and
who give of themselves and of the human and material resources of their companies to those things that encourage
community, that uphold human life, that lift hearts and hopes,
and hold together the life of the city;

artists who bring together shape and form and color ... musi-
cians who harmonize ideas and melodies and voices . . . poets
and writers who weave words with clarity and emotion — all
of whom feed our souls and lift our spirits;

teachers in school and church, interpreters of ideas who help us
hold onto and hold together the best of human thought and
discovery;

diplomats and negotiators who hold together international relationships, friendships, agreements, treaties, cease-fires in the
service of good will and reconciliation;

military personnel and law enforcement officers who place themselves in danger in order to hold together the defense of our
nation and our security at home;

physicians who hold together the working of body and mind in
health and wholeness;

those who work unseen and often unappreciated behind the
scenes to hold together all manner of enterprises without
whom institutions, organizations, industries could hardly
function, if at all.

And now, O God, hold us together we pray as we seek to be your
people in this place, that the ministry of this church might be a
ministry of holding together people whose lives are tossed and torn
by illness and grief, by hunger and poverty, by violence and enmity,
by the struggle to provide for their families against forces that would
seem to any of us overwhelming. Be especially with those for whom
Thanksgiving this year will be difficult and fraught with worry as
they face the holiday season and the new year anxious about jobs

lost or in jeopardy. Help us to know what we can do as a church and as a city to care for the children and families of our community — their minds and bodies and spirits. Grant that, in the spirit and in the name of Jesus Christ, we who bear his name might seek to hold together in hospitality and peace and mutual respect the various communities of faith in our city. So might we together allow the light of our respective faiths to shine upon the common way that, with good will, we would journey together along our different paths. All these our prayers we offer in the name of him in whom all things are reconciled and held together, even Jesus Christ our Lord, who taught us to pray . . .

Amen.

A Thanksgiving Prayer

Have no anxiety about anything, but in everything by prayer and supplication with thanksgiving let your requests be made known to God. (Phil. 4:6, RSV)

Let us pray: Eternal God, you have made all things by your power, you rule the world and redeem women and men, and you are more wonderful in your majesty than we can know, and in your mercy than we can understand. We worship you: author, preserver, redeemer of all life.

We thank you for the life and joy of your whole creation, for the rhythm of its seasons, for the rigor of its disciplines, for the miracle of abundance by which we are sustained, for creatures great and small in whom you have revealed your life-giving power, for the warmth of the day and the quiet of the night, for the work that follows rest and rest that follows work, and for all the alternations by which you temper the rigors of life to human frailty.

We thank you for the fellowship of women and men under your providence, for the structure of life by which you have ordained that none of us, even though we may dwell alone, should live alone. We thank you for our families and our responsibilities toward each other . . . for our communities of common interest and work and faith in which we discipline each other in our mutual tasks . . . for the large communities of destiny into which we are bound in our nations . . . and finally for our common dependence on and responsibility to the family of nations. We thank you for every discipline which teaches us that if we try to gain, seize, or master our life we lose it, but if we offer life in the Master's service to any of his children, we gain it.

Eternal God, you are the source and end of our life and the light also of our pilgrimage: grant your grace so that the good in us may prevail over the evil, so that everything in us may be brought into harmony with your will, and so that we may be enabled to live in compassion and justice with our neighbors and fellow citizens of this planet.

O Lord, you are the confidence of all the ends of the earth and the refuge of your children in all generations; enlarge our faith and love so that we may pray truly for needs beyond our own. We pray for our country and its leaders: keep them on the paths of justice and peace. We pray for those throughout the world who call on your name and for all who are your ministers of mercy, that each may serve you more truly according to his or her vocation. We pray for those who work with their hands, that they may know the dignity of their labor. We pray for those who care for the young, that they may not cause any of the little ones to stumble.

As we look upon a world in which too often simmering suspicion and mistrust spill over into violence, we lift before you the distressed and dispossessed, grieving and anguished souls who are victims of the storms and cruelties of war. We pray for the families and loved ones of those whose lives have been the sacrifices exacted by the terrors between and within nations: stand with them in their grief and draw them close to yourself by your strong compassion and sustaining presence. We entreat you to bring to a swift conclusion the wounding of the human spirit and the destruction of life and homeland that are the terrible price war extracts from all of us.

We know, Lord God, that war is not your will for the children of earth. We hardly know how to pray about it except to plead that, in a world too eager to study war and resort to violence, you will in your providence grant that peace may overcome enmity, and that your justice and righteousness may guide us in and beyond hostile environments and destructive engagements. We pray that your Spirit who guides us in our praying may help us to pray honestly and earnestly for our enemies and those who wish us harm and do us injury, that in your time and within your purpose reconciliation may come that is born of your own reconciliation of the world to yourself in Jesus Christ.

So rekindle among the nations in these days a renewed commitment to the things that make for peace, to the seeking and doing justice that acts with mercy, and that resolves to live with and toward one another with understanding and good will.

O Lord, save us from heedlessness in a world full of sorrow, and from self-righteousness, for in our world the sins of even the most wicked trace some kinship with the sins of even the most righteous. Cover us all by your mercy, and lead us to a fuller understanding of your will.

O God, you have taught us to pray for the coming of your kingdom on this earth: give us grace to build our communities after the fashion of your kingdom, to set no boundaries about them which you would not set, to quiet the tumult within them by love and compassion, and to work more diligently for the better concord within them. All this we pray because our final security lies in the city which has foundations, whose builder and maker is God.

And now, O God our Father, in this Thanksgiving season our prayers turn to those from whom we are absent, but whom we hold and name in our hearts. We commit their lives and our own lives to your care, confident that your promise to Jacob at Bethel is your word to us as well: "Know that I am with you and will keep you wherever you go." So then whether we are at home or far away, with family and friends or alone among strangers, your presence sustains us. Whether we are confident or anxious, happy or heartbroken, your promise undergirds us. Whether we acknowledge you or not, you will not forsake us: your mercy shall be greater than our self-will, your faith in us stronger than our denial of you. Whether we have too much or too little wealth for our own good; whether our reputation is better than our soul, or our soul better than our reputation; whether we know much of the world's wisdom or very little, you will walk beside us and guide us until at last the light of your truth and grace illumines our minds, clarifies our understanding, and directs our hearts to their true home in you. Then we shall be your children in fact and in faith, and wherever we may be, we shall be with you. Wherefore we praise your name, O God: Father, Son, Holy Spirit, one God forever, world without end.

Amen.

A Funeral Prayer of
Thanksgiving and Intercession

Eternal God, out of a love that transcends our best understanding, you call us into being; you cradle us in mercy and mystery; you give purpose to our living, light to our eyes, wisdom to our mind; you create us for an eternal destiny. By your providence you walk beside us all our days; you keep us ever in your care; when we lose our grip on life and our eyes close in death, we fall into your everlasting arms, and you open our eyes again upon your kingdom and your face. What shall we ask that you have not given? What shall we render save obedience, love, and praise?

You have set your glory upon the heavens, and your image in the human creature. You have made us for yourself, and our lives are restless until they find their rest in you. We praise your name that all our days arise and set in you, O God. May we take them from your hand with gratitude, fashion them with courage, and give them back with joy, confident that for time and for eternity our lives are "hid with Christ in God."

We give thanks not only for the days you have given us, O God our Creator, but also for your gift of grace for the living of our days. You have loved us into life, and all our days you have not grown weary of loving us. You have given us your word of promise to go before us to illumine our way and to carry us along that way. You have given us your holy law to shape our lives and character according to your will. You have given us your word of judgment to correct us and to remind us to whom we belong. You have given us your Word made flesh to dwell among us, even Jesus Christ, Emmanuel — God with us, the concrete expression of your love that never fails and that, before it will be anything else than love, will let itself be nailed to a cross and laid in a tomb, and even then will be love undying and invincible. You have set us in homes, in families, in churches, and among friends whose care and comradeship point beyond themselves to that perfect fellowship and care in which we are bound to you for time and for eternity.

Your mercies, Eternal God, are from everlasting to everlasting. We confess that our days are brief and fleeting. Upon our human love we build our lives and they come to an end. But you remain, with whom is no passing away, whose faithfulness endures before creation and beyond resurrection. We confess with joy and gladness that you are able to, and that you will keep that which we have committed unto you against that day when we walk through the valley of the shadow of death. That you are our keeper, eternally, presently, and surely is the undergirding strength of our faith in life and death and destiny.

We praise your name for Jesus Christ, who dwelt among us as the Word made flesh, God with us in person, to taste our joy, to suffer our sorrow, to embody for us your steadfast love, in whose care we dwell, and they dwell also whom we love now beyond the limit of sight.

*[Here particular prayers of thanksgiving are offered
for the life of the deceased.]*

And now, O God, come unto us all within the mystery and reality of death that frightens and unsteadies us, and that leaves hearts heavy and faith shaken. Let us hear again your own promise and assurance in the depths of our sadness and spiritual need. So shall we rest our grief in your faithfulness, our pain in your tender mercy, our lives and the life of our beloved in your steadfast love that never lets us go.

Remind us also of your gracious and faithful ruling, accompanying, preserving, redeeming of our lives and of each life. Your gift he/she was whom we have loved. These loved ones and friends by whom we are surrounded are your gifts of grace to strengthen us in time of need. And from you, through you, and to you are all things. Let us not imagine, therefore, that we are exiled from your loving presence, but rather are enfolded and held secure within your everlasting arms.

Lead us, O God, to seek the meaning and purpose of our lives neither in light nor in darkness, but in your steadfast love, whence are all beginnings and all endings. And so fill our hearts with trust in you that by night and by day, at all times and in all seasons, we may without fear commit ourselves and those whom we love to your eternal keeping, to your never-failing care, to your steadfast love for this life and for the life to come. We offer our prayer in the name of Jesus Christ our Lord, who reigns with you, O Father, and the Holy Spirit, one God forever, world without end.

Amen.

In both form and theology, this prayer reflects the prayer offered by Balmer H. Kelly, Dean of the Faculty, on November 19, 1966, at the memorial service for James A. Jones, President of Union Theological Seminary in Virginia. Members of the seminary faculty and administration planned and conducted the service along with John S. Brown, pastor of Ginter Park Presbyterian Church next to the seminary campus in Richmond.

Marked by biblical affirmation, theological depth, and pastoral care, the service ministered to our lives personally and to the life of the community. Indeed, many of us who were then students have since acknowledged how that service focused, and continues to shape, our own understanding and conduct of the church's ministry at times of death and grief.

Each element of the service contributed to its faithfulness to the best of Reformed worship and to the service's overall effectiveness. The prayer demonstrated that women and men of "all sorts and conditions" still need words spoken and witness borne in affirmation and assurance of God's unfailing mercy and steadfast love. There was no sermon. Rather, it was in the prayer that we heard of "the unsearchable riches of Christ" and in which we found "grace to help in time of need."

Here was a clear acknowledgment that, from our pastor, we deserve to hear and understand our existence as from God, life lived before and in response to God, our lives held and upheld both presently and eternally by God's encompassing presence and sovereign grace. Such comfort and assurance come from a deep awareness that life is finite, but not haphazard; that, come heaven or hell, God is with us and for us; that "neither death, nor life . . . nor anything else in all creation, will be able to separate us from the love of God in Christ Jesus our Lord."

Just so did a particular memorial service, thoughtfully planned and conducted, confirm the faith of that worshiping community, and give valued assurance to eager but inexperienced women and men whose ministries it has helped to guide.